CLASSIC SERMONS
ON THE
NAMES OF GOD

KREGEL CLASSIC SERMONS Series

Classic Sermons on the Apostle Peter

Classic Sermons on the Attributes of God

Classic Sermons on the Birth of Christ

Classic Sermons on Christian Service

Classic Sermons on the Cross of Christ

Classic Sermons on Faith and Doubt

Classic Sermons on Family and Home

Classic Sermons on Heaven and Hell

Classic Sermons on Hope

Classic Sermons on Judas Iscariot

Classic Sermons on the Miracles of Christ

Classic Sermons on the Names of God

Classic Sermons on Overcoming Fear

Classic Sermons on Praise

Classic Sermons on Prayer

Classic Sermons on the Prodigal Son

Classic Sermons on the Resurrection of Christ

Classic Sermons on Revival and Spiritual Renewal

Classic Sermons on the Second Coming and
Other Prophetic Themes

Classic Sermons on the Sovereignty of God

Classic Sermons on Spiritual Warfare

Classic Sermons on Suffering

Classic Sermons on Worship

CLASSIC SERMONS
ON THE
NAMES OF GOD

Compiled by
Warren W. Wiersbe

kregel
PUBLICATIONS

Grand Rapids, MI 49501

Classic Sermons on the Names of God, compiled by Warren
W. Wiersbe. Copyright © 1993 by Kregel Publications, a
division of Kregel, Inc., P. O. Box 2607, Grand Rapids,
MI 49501. All rights reserved.

Cover and Book Design: Alan G. Hartman

Library of Congress Cataloging-in-Publication Data

Classic Sermons on the names of God / compiled by Warren
W. Wiersbe.
    p.   cm.— (Kregel classic sermons series)
  Includes index.

  1. God—Name—Sermons. 2. Sermons, English.
3. Sermons, American. I. Wiersbe, Warren W. II. Series:
Kregel classic sermons series.

BT180.N2C53   1993   231—dc20   92-39330
                                            CIP

ISBN   0-8254-4052-1 (pbk.)

            2 3 4 5 Printing/Year 97 96

        Printed in the United States of America

CONTENTS

5

SCRIPTURE TEXT INDEX

PREFACE

THE *KREGEL CLASSIC SERMONS SERIES* is an attempt to assemble and publish meaningful sermons from master preachers about significant themes.

These are *sermons*, not essays or chapters taken from books about themes. Not all of these sermons could be called "great," but all of them are *meaningful*. They apply the truths of the Bible to the needs of the human heart which is something that all effective preaching must do.

While some are better known than others, all of the preachers, whose sermons I have selected, had important ministries and were highly respected in their day. The fact that a sermon is included in this volume does not mean that either the compiler or the publisher agrees with or endorses everything that the man did, preached, or wrote. The sermon is here because it has a valued contribution to make.

These are sermons about *significant* themes. The pulpit is no place to play with trivia. The preacher has thirty minutes in which to help mend broken hearts, change defeated lives, and save lost souls; and one can never accomplish this demanding ministry by distributing homiletical tidbits. In these difficult days, we do not need "clever" pulpiteers who discuss the times; we need dedicated ambassadors who will preach the eternities.

The reading of these sermons can enrich your own spiritual life. The studying of them can enrich your own skills as an interpreter and expounder of God's truth. However God uses these sermons in your own life and ministry, my prayer is that His Church around the world will be encouraged and strengthened.

WARREN W. WIERSBE

Jehovah Shammah—A Glorious Name for the New Year

Charles Haddon Spurgeon (1834-1892) is undoubtedly the most famous minister of modern times. Converted in 1850, he united with the Baptists and soon began to preach in various places. He became pastor of the Baptist church in Waterbeach in 1851, and three years later he was called to the decaying Park Street Church, London. Within a short time, the work began to prosper, a new church was built and dedicated in 1861, and Spurgeon became London's most popular preacher. In 1855, he began to publish his sermons weekly; and today they make up the fifty-seven volumes of *The Metropolitan Tabernacle Pulpit*. He founded a pastor's college and several orphanages.

This sermon is taken from *The Metropolitan Tabernacle Pulpit*, Volume 37.

Charles Haddon Spurgeon

1

JEHOVAH SHAMMAH—A GLORIOUS NAME FOR THE NEW YEAR

The name of the city from that day shall be, The Lord is there [or in Hebrew "Jehovah Shammah"] (Ezekiel 48:35).

THESE WORDS MAY be used as a test as well as a text. They may serve for examination as well as consolation, and at the beginning of a year they may fulfill this useful double purpose. In any case, they are full of marrow and fatness to those whose spiritual taste is purified. It is esteemed by the prophet to be the highest blessing that could come upon a city that its name should be, "JEHOVAH SHAMMAH, The Lord is there." Even Jerusalem, in its best estate, would have this for its crowning blessing: nothing could exceed this. Do *we* reckon the presence of the Lord to be the greatest of blessings? If in any gathering, even of the humblest people, the Lord God is known to be present in a peculiarly gracious manner, should *we* make a point of being there? Very much depends upon our answer to these queries.

Doubtless many would be greatly pleased if there were no God at all; for in their hearts they say, "No God." God is not to them a father, a friend, a trust, a treasure. If they were to speak from their hearts, and could hope for a satisfactory answer, they would ask, "Whither can I flee from His presence?" If a spot could be found wherein there would be no God, what a fine building speculation might be made there! Millions would emigrate to "No God's land," and would feel at ease as soon as they trod its godless shore. There they could do just as they liked, without fear of future reckoning. Now, friend, if you would fain escape from the presence of God, your state is clearly revealed by that fact. There can be no heaven for you; for heaven is where the Lord's presence is fullness of joy. If you could be happy to be far off from God, I must tell you what your fate will be. You are now going away from God in your heart and desire, and at last the great Judge of all will say to you, "Depart, ye cursed"; and you will then be driven from the presence of the Lord, and from the glory of His power.

I know that there is a company who can truly say that they feel happy only when they are conscious that God is with them. The place where they meet with the Lord is very dear and precious to them because of His unveilings. The memory of holy convocations is sweet because the Lord was among them. They would not care to go where God is not. If there were a place forsaken of God, however exciting and full of merriment men might think it, they would not be found among its guests. Where we cannot enjoy God's company we will not go. Our motto is: "With God, anywhere. Without God, nowhere." In Him we live, and move, and have our being; and, therefore, it would be death to us to be apart from God. Without God we should be without hope. Ah, my dear friend! Whatever your difficulties, and trials, and sorrows, all is well with you if God is your delight, and His presence your joy. But, however high your temporal enjoyments may rise, it is all wrong with you if you can rest away from the God of grace. The child must be in a sad state of heart when he does not care to have his father's approving smile. Things must be terribly wrong with any creature when it can be content to walk contrary to its Creator. Nothing but the corruption of the heart could permit any man to be at ease away from God.

Will you permit these thoughts to saturate you for a little space? I have spoken them with the desire that each one of us may ask himself, "Is the presence of God my delight?" If so, I am His, and He will be with me. On the contrary, Is the presence of God a matter of indifference, or even of dread? Then my condition is one of guilt, disease, and danger. May the Lord, of His infinite mercy, set me right!

This much may stand as a preface; but it must not be treated as most prefaces are, namely, left unread, or glanced over and forgotten. I pray you, carry it with you all along.

I. Now kindly notice that, according to our text,

The Presence of God Is the Glory of the Most Glorious Place.

The prophet Ezekiel has been telling us many remarkable things which I shall not attempt to explain to you; and my chief reason for not doing so is the fact that I do not understand them. If I could open up every dark saying, it is not just now the time to go into an explanation of all the sublime mysteries which were seen by the eagle eye of Ezekiel, for I seek present, practical edification; and this we can gain in an easier way. It is clear from the text, that when God shall bless His ancient people, and restore them to their land, and the temple shall be rebuilt, and all the glory of the latter days shall arrive, this will still be the peculiar glory of it all, that *"the Lord is there."* The prophet works up a climax, and closes his book of prophecy with these glorious words, *"the Lord is there."*

What a glorious state this world was in at the very first, *in the age of Paradise*, for the Lord was there! Our glorious Creator, having taken the first days of the week to make the world, and fit it up for man, did not bring forward His dear child until the house was built and furnished, and supplied for his use and happiness. He did not put him in the garden to dress it till the roses were blooming and the fruits were ripe. When the table was furnished He introduced the guest by saying, "Let us make man in our image, after our likeness." The Lord put man not in an unreclaimed plot of soil where he must hunger till he could produce a harvest; but into an Eden of delights where he was at home with creatures of every sort to attend him. He had not to water dry lands, nor need he thirst himself, for four rivers flowed through his royal domain, rippling over sands of gold. I might say much of that fair garden of innocence and bliss, but the best thing I could say would be *the Lord was there.* "The Lord God walked in the garden in the cool of the day," and communed with man; and man, being innocent, held high converse with his condescending Maker. The topstone of the bliss of Paradise was this all-comprehending privilege—"the Lord is there."

Alas! that has vanished. Withered are the bowers of Eden; the trail of the serpent is over all landscapes, however fair. Yet days of mercy came, and God's saints in divers places found choice spots where they could converse with heaven. *In the first days* our gracious God spoke with His chosen ones in their daily walk, as Enoch; or under the oak, as Abraham; or by the brook, as Jacob; or before the bush, as Moses; or near the city wall, as Joshua. Wherever it might be, the place became to them the gate of heaven, for the Lord was there. Amid a torrent of sin and sorrow, you may cross the stream of time upon the stepping-stones of the places marked "JEHOVAH SHAMMAH." The Lord's delights were with the sons of men, and to them nothing brought such bliss as to find that still the Lord would be mindful of man and visit him.

In the days when God had called out unto Himself a chosen nation, *He revealed Himself at Sinai*, when the mountain was altogether on a smoke, and even Moses said, "I do exceedingly fear and quake." Well might he feel a holy awe, for the Lord was there. I will not dwell upon the glory of the tabernacle that was pitched in the wilderness with its costly furniture and its instructive rites, for after all, the glory of the tabernacle was that the Lord was there. A bright light shone between the wings of the cherubim, and so the Psalmist in after days spoke unto the Lord saying, "Thou that dwellest between the cherubims shine forth." Above the sacred tent was the pillar of fire by night and the pillar of cloud by day—an emblem of the constant presence of God, for all through the wilderness His glorious marchings were in the center of the armies of His Israel. The desert sand glowed with the blaze of the present Deity. No spot on earth was so like to heaven's high courts as that wilderness wherein there was no way, wherein the Lord Himself led His people like a flock. Holy was Horeb, for the Lord was there.

Then were the days of Israel's espousals, for the Most High tabernacled among her tribes, and made them "a people near unto Him."

In Canaan itself the days of sorrow came when the nation went after other gods, and the Lord became a stranger in the land. *When He returned, and delivered His people by the judges*, then the nations knew that Israel could not be trampled on, for the Lord was there. *This was the glory of David's reign*. Then the Lord made bare His arm, and the enemies of His chosen were driven like snow from the bleak sides of Salmon when the rough blast carries it away. This was the shout of the joyful people, "The Lord of hosts is with us: the God of Jacob is our refuge." Never were the hills of Judah more fruitful, nor the vales of Sharon more peaceful, nor the homes of Israel more restful, nor the sons of Zion more valiant, than when to the harp of David the song was raised, "They have seen thy goings, O God; even the goings of my God, my King, in the sanctuary. This is the hill which God desireth to dwell in; yea, the Lord shall dwell in it forever."

You remember how, in after ages, when Solomon was crowned and his reign of peace had been inaugurated, *he built for God a temple* adorned with gold and precious stones, and all manner of cunning work of the artificer; but it was not that glittering roof, it was not those massive pillars of brass in the forefront, it was not the hecatombs of bullocks whose blood was poured forth at the altar which were the glory of the temple of Mount Zion. Beautiful for situation, it was the joy of the whole earth; but its glory lay in this—"God is in the midst of her; she shall not be moved: God shall help her, and that right early." The excellence of the temple was seen when, on the opening day, the Lord revealed Himself, and "the cloud filled the house of the Lord, so that the priests could not stand to minister because of the cloud: for the glory of the Lord had filled the house of the Lord." Little remains for man to do when in very deed the Lord dwells in the midst of His saints. Apart from priests and ceremonies, that place is sacred wherein the Lord Most High has His abode. Say of any place "Jehovah-shammah, the Lord is there," and be it tent or temple, you have spoken glorious things of it.

I almost tremble while I remind you of the truest temple of God—*the body of our Lord.* The nearest approach of Godhead to our manhood was when there was found, wrapped in swaddling bands and lying in a manger, that child who was born, that Son who was given, whose name was called "Wonderful, Counselor, The mighty God, The everlasting Father, The Prince of Peace." As for thee, O Bethlehem, favored above all the towns of earth, out of thee He came, who is Immanuel, God with us! Verily thy name is Jehovah-shammah. All along, through thirty years and more of holy labor, ending in a shameful death, God was in Christ reconciling the world unto Himself. In the gloom of Gethsemane, among those somber olives, when Jesus bowed, and in His prayer sweat, as it were, great drops of blood falling to the ground, He was "seen of angels" as the Son of God bearing human sin. Speak of Gethsemane, and we tell you God was there. Before Herod, and Pilate, and Caiaphas, and on the cross—the Lord was there. Though in a sense there was the hiding of God, and Jesus cried, "Why hast thou forsaken me?" Yet in the deepest sense Jehovah was there, bruising the great sacrifice. The thick darkness made a veil for the Lord of glory, and behind it He that made all things bowed His head and said, "It is finished." God was in Christ Jesus on the cross, and we, beholding Him, feel that we have seen the Father. O Calvary, we say of thee, "The Lord is there."

Here I might fitly close, for we can mount no higher; but yet we could not afford to leave out those other dwellings of the Invisible Spirit, who still by His presence makes holy places even in this unholy world. We have to remind you that God is the glory of the most glorious living thing that has been on the face of the earth since our Lord was here. And what is that? I answer, Jesus is gone; the prophets are gone; and we have no temple, no human priest, no material holy of holies.

Jesus, where'er thy people meet,
There they behold thy mercy-seat:
Where'er they seek thee, thou art found,
And every place is hallowed ground.

And yet there is a special place where God dwells among men, and that is *in His church.* He has but one—one church, chosen by eternal election, redeemed by precious blood, called out by the Holy Spirit, and quickened into newness of life—this as a whole is the dwelling-place of the covenant God. Because God is in this church, therefore the gates of hell shall not prevail against her. "The Lord is there" might be said of the church in all ages. I have seen the crypts and underground chapels of the catacombs, and it made one feel that they were glorious places, when we remembered that the Lord God was there, by His Spirit, with His suffering people. When holy hymn and psalm and solemn prayer went up from the very bowels of the earth, from men who were hunted to the death by their foes—the Lord was there. In those dreary excavations, unvisited by sunlight and wholesome air, God was as He was not in the palaces of kings, and is not in the cathedrals of priests. In this land of ours, when a few people met together, here and there, to hear the gospel and to worship, they made cottages, caves, and hollows in the woods, to be "holiness unto the Lord." Ay, and when crowds met beneath your gospel oaks, or gathered together by the hillside to listen to the pure word of grace, the Lord was there, and souls were saved and sanctified. When the Puritans solemnly conversed together of the things of God, and held their little conventicles for fear of their adversaries—God was there. On Scotland's bleak moors and mosses, when the covenanters gathered in the darkness and the storm, for fear of Claverhouse and his dragoons—God was there. Those who wrote in those days tell us that they never knew such season in days of peace as they enjoyed among the hills, amid the heather, or by the brook-side; for Jehovah Shammah, the Lord was there.

And so onward, to this very day, wheresoever the chosen of God lift up holy hands and worship Him, whether it be in cathedral or in barn, beneath the blue sky or beneath a thatched roof, anywhere and everywhere when the heart is right, and the soul adores the living Lord, this is the special glory of the place, that "Jehovah Shammah, the Lord is there."

Flying forward, as with a dove's wing, to the future that is drawing near, we reflect on the truth that there is to be *a millennial age*—a time of glory, and peace, and joy, and truth, and righteousness. But what is to be the glory of it? Why this, "Jehovah Shammah, the Lord is there!" The Lord Jesus Christ will come and begin His personal reign on earth among His ancients. In like manner as He went up into heaven, and the disciples saw Him, so will He descend a second time to be seen here among men; and His glorious presence shall fashion the golden age, the thousand years of peace. Then shall the nations shout, "The Lord is come." What hallelujahs will then rise to heaven! Welcome, welcome, son of God! How will all His faithful ones rejoice with joy unspeakable and sing and sing again; for now the day of their reward has come, and they shall shine forth as the sun in the kingdom of their Father! In all the glory of the latter days everything is wrapped up in this one word, "the Lord is there."

> Oh, come, thou Dayspring, come and cheer
> Our spirits by thine advent here;
> Disperse the gloomy clouds of night,
> And death's dark shadows put to flight!
> Rejoice, Rejoice! Immanuel
> Shall come to thee, O Israel!

Up yonder, whither many of our beloved ones have already gone; up yonder, within that gate of pearl where eye cannot as yet see. What is it that makes *heaven*, with all its supreme delights? Not harps of angels, nor blaze of seraphim; but this one fact, "the Lord is there." What must it be to be with God? O soul that loves Him, what will your fullness of pleasure be when you shall dwell with Him for whom your soul is hungering and thirsting! What joy to be "forever with the Lord"! This perfect bliss may be ours this very day. We little know how near we are to our glorification with our Lord. The veil is very thin that parts the sanctified from the glorified.

> One gentle sigh, the soul awakes:
> We scarce can say "He's gone,"
> Before the ransomed spirit takes
> Its mansion near the throne.

The joy and glory of those divine mansions is that "the Lord is there." Heaven's loftiest peak shines forever in this clear light—The Lord God and the Lamb are the light thereof: "the Lord is there."

Enough of this. I have proved my point, that the glory of the most glorious place is that "the Lord is there."

II. Suffer me for a few minutes to speak to you upon another point:

The Presence of God Is the Best Privilege of His Church.

It is her glory that "the Lord is there." Note this, and mark it well. Brethren, we as a church have grown to great numbers, and we are not deficient either in gifts or in graces, or in work for our Lord; but let me solemnly remind you always that our chief, our only strength, must always lie in this—"the Lord is there." If the Lord should depart from us, as He has gone from churches which are now apostate, what an abyss opens before us! If He should take His Holy Spirit from us, even as the glory departed from the temple at Jerusalem, then our ruin would become a thing to mention with dread, a case to be quoted for a warning to future generations. O Lord, our God, take not thy flight! Abide with us, we pray thee! Our only hope lies in thy making the place of thy feet glorious among us.

If the Lord be among us, the consequences will be, first, *the conservation of true doctrine.* The true God is not with a lie; He will not give His countenance to falsehood. Those who preach other than according to His Word, abide not under His blessing but are in great danger of His curse. If any man speak another gospel (which is not another, but there be some that trouble us), God is not with him, and any transient prosperity which he may enjoy will be blown away as the chaff. God is with those who speak the truth faithfully, hold it devoutly, believe it firmly, and live upon it as their daily bread. May it always be said of this church, "the Lord is there," and therefore they are sound in the faith, reverent toward Holy Scripture, and zealous for the honor of Christ! Trust-deeds and confessions of faith are useful in their way, even as laws are useful to society; but as laws cannot secure obedience to themselves, so articles of belief cannot create faith or secure honesty; and to men without conscience, they are not worth the paper they are written upon. No subscription to articles can keep out the unscrupulous. Wolves leap into the fold however carefully you watch the door. The fact is, the most of people say, "Yes, that doctrine is in the creed, and is not to be denied; but you need not preach it. Put it on the shelf as an ornament, and let us hear no more about it." Truth must be written on the heart as well as in the book. If the Lord be among His people, they will cling to the eternal verities and love the doctrine of the cross, not by force of law, but because divine truth is the life of their souls.

Where God is present, *the preservation of purity* will be found. The church is nothing if it is not holy. It is worse— it is a den of thieves. Setting the seal of its pestilent example upon evil living, it becomes the servant of Satan and the destroyer of souls. Who is to keep the church pure? None but God Himself. If the Lord is there, holiness will abound, and fruits of the Spirit will be seen on all sides; but if the Lord be once withdrawn, then flesh and blood will rule, and bring forth corruption after its own manner; and the church will become a synagogue of formalists. Pray, my brethren, continually, that the Lord may dwell in our Zion, to maintain us in all holy obedience and purity of life.

Where God is, there is *the constant renewal of vitality.* A dead church is a reeking Golgotha, a breeding-place of evils, a home of devils. The tombs may be newly white-washed, but they are nonetheless open sepulchers, haunts of unclean spirits. A church all alive is a little heaven, the resort of angels, the temple of the Holy Spirit. In some of our churches everybody seems to be a little colder than everybody else. The members are holy icicles. A general frost has paralyzed everybody; and though some are colder than others, yet all are below zero. There are no flowing rills of refreshment, but everything is bound hard and fast with the frost of indifference. Oh, that the Lord would send forth His wind and melt the glaciers! Oh, that the Spirit of God would chase winter out of every heart and every church! No human power can keep a church from the frostbite which numbs and kills. Except the Lord be there, growth, life, warmth—are all impossible. Ye that make mention of the Lord, keep not silence and give Him no rest, but cry day and night to Him, "O Lord, abide with us. Go forth with our armies. Make us to be the living children of the living God"!

When the Lord is there, next, *there is continuing power*. With God there is power in the ministry, power in prayer, power in all holy work. We may do a vast deal of work, and yet nothing may come of it; and, on the other hand, we may only be able to do comparatively little, and yet great results may flow therefrom for results depend not on the quantity of the machinery but on the presence of the Lord.

Do you not all know persons who are not peculiarly gifted and yet are eminently useful? You do not remark anything about them that is specially noticeable, and yet their whole career enlists attention by its power. Their words tell for there is character behind them. A consistent life gives force to a plain testimony. It is not so much what is said as who says it. But that is not all; God Himself is at the back of the man who is living for Him. He causes him to speak in His name so that none of his words fall to the ground. Is it not said of the godly, "His leaf also shall not wither; and whatsoever he doeth shall prosper"? This is so with every church where the Lord abides. His presence makes it a power with its children and adherents, a power with the neighborhood, and a power with the age. Its example, its testimony, its effort tells. God uses it, and therefore it answers its end. The power is with God; but the church is the instrument by which that power exercises itself. He uses a living people for the display of living power, and He gives to them both life and power, more and more abundantly. As we desire power with which to labor for God, we must pray that the God of power will remain in our midst.

Furthermore, whenever it can be said of an assembly, "the Lord is there," *unity will be created and fostered.* Show me a church that quarrels, a church that is split up into cliques, a church that is divided with personal ambitions, contrary doctrines, and opposing schemes, and I am sure that the Lord is not there. Where there are envyings, jealousies, suspicions, backbitings, and dislikes, I know that the Holy Dove, Who hates confusion, has taken His flight. God is love, and He will only dwell where love reigns. He is the God of peace and will not endure strife. The children of God should be knit together. It would indeed be a shameful sight should children of His family fall out, and chide, and fight. Saints who dwell with God love each other "with a pure heart, fervently." Some professors act as if they hated each other: I may not say, "with a pure heart," but I will say, "fervently." Where God is present the church is edified in love and grows up, like a building fitly framed together, to be a holy temple in the Lord. Oh, for more of this unity!

Where the Lord is *there is sure to be happiness.* What meetings we have when the Lord is here! It is a prayer meeting; but when you have said that, you have not fully described it, for it is far more. It was an unusual meeting for prayer, for, God being there, every prayer was spoken into His ear, and all the desires and petitions of the saints were prompted by His Holy Spirit. Why, the very room was lit up with the glory of the Lord; and whether we were in heaven or not we could hardly tell. What happy times we have in preaching the Word of the Lord when God's own presence is realized! His paths drop fatness. What joyous seasons we have frequently enjoyed at the communion table! The provision is but bread and wine; but when, by faith, we perceive the real and spiritual presence of the Lord Jesus Christ, in the breaking of the bread we eat His flesh, and in the fruit of the vine we drink His blood. When we have gathered in the Lord's presence we have sung—

> No beams of cedar or of fir
> Can with thy courts on earth compare;
> And here we wait, until thy love
> Raise us to nobler seats above.

At the Master's table I have often been so blest that I would not have exchanged places with Gabriel. The Lord was there: what more could I desire? Joy, delight, rapture, ecstasy—what word shall I use?—all these have waited around the table of fellowship as musicians at a king's banquet. If God be there, our heaven is there.

III. I shall now close by noticing, in the third place, that since this presence of God is the glory of the most glorious place, and the choice privilege of the most privileged, it is our exceeding joy:

The Presence of the Lord Is Our Delight in Every Place.

We will think of *our own dear homes*. What a delightful family we belong to if it can be said of our house, "Jehovah Shammah, the Lord is there"! Has it a thatched roof and a stone floor? What matters? The father of the family lives near to God, and his wife rejoices to be his fellow-helper in prayer while the children grow up to honest toil and honorable service. Assuredly that cottage home is dear to God and becomes a place where angels come and go. Because God is there, every window looks toward the Celestial City. It is a comfort that we need not go across the road to morning prayer or step out every evening to worship, for we are priests ourselves and have a family altar at home whereon the incense burns both morning and night. We talk not of Morning Prayer and vespers, but we glory that "the Lord is there" when we bow the knee as a household. What is more delightful than to gather round the family hearth, to hear the Scriptures read, and listen to the senior as he talks to the younger ones of what God has done for him and what the Lord is

waiting to give to all who trust Him? Free from all for-
mality, family prayer makes a house a temple, a family a
church, and every day a holy day. Truly, I may say of
families of this kind, wherever they dwell, that it is "none
other but the house of God, and it is the very gate of
heaven"; for "the Lord is there." Friend, is God in your
house? If it has no family prayer, it has no roof to it.
There is no true joy in domestic life unless the Lord be
there. All else is fiction; God alone is true delight. I charge
you, if your homes are not such that God could come to
them, set your houses in order and say, "As for me and
my house, we will serve the Lord." Will you dare to dwell
where God could not lodge with you? May all men say of
your home, "The Lord is there"!

Here is *a Christian who lives alone*, apart altogether
from family life. All his dear ones are dead or far away. In
his lone chamber, when he bows his knee in secret prayer,
or whenever he takes his walk abroad to meditate, if he
be indeed a true lover of the Lord Jesus, "the Lord is
there." Wherever the believer's lot is cast, if he lives in
fellowship with Christ, he may say of his quiet room, or of
the garden-walk, or even of the stable or the loft, "Jehovah Shammah, the Lord is there." Many a humble garret
is a right royal residence! for "the Lord is there." Better
Paul's inner dungeon at Philippi with his feet fast in the
stocks and the presence of the Lord, than the grandest
apartments of Cæsar's palace and an unknown God. The
Lord is very gracious to His lonely ones. They can say,
"And yet I am not alone, for the Father is with me." Put
you in a hospital or in a workhouse, what matters it, if
Jehovah is at your side to cheer you?

Some of us can bear witness that we have had the
nearest approaches of God to our souls in *times of intoler-
able pain* and even in seasons of intense depression of
spirit as to earthly things. "I was brought low, and the
Lord helped me," said David; and we can say the same.
The Lord has said, "When thou passest through the waters, I will be with thee"; as much as to say, "If I am not
with thee anywhere else, I will be with thee then." In the
furnace one like unto the Son of God was seen. If Shadrach,

Meshach, and Abednego never had that glorious fourth person in their company before, they had Him when they were cast into the midst of the glowing coals. Jehovah-shammah makes a seven-times-heated furnace a pleasant arbor. We may say of the refining fire, and of the threshing-floor, and of the oil-press, God has been there. In the time of trouble He has been a very present help. One might almost say, "Send me back to my prison again," as one did say who lost God's presence after he had gained his liberty. One might well cry, "Ah! let me have back my pain if I may again overflow with the joy of the Lord's presence."

Dear friends, I thank God that you and I know what it is to enjoy the presence of God in a great many different ways. *When two or three of the people of God meet together*, and talk to one another about the things of God, the Lord is never away. You remember that blessed text, "They that feared the Lord spoke often one to another." They had holy talks about heavenly things. It was such sweet conversation that the Lord Himself turned eaves-dropper and hearkened and heard. What He heard pleased Him so well that He there and then made a note of it; yea, and wrote it down, and ordered that "a book of remembrance" should be preserved "for them that feared the Lord, and that thought upon his name." Was not this sure evidence of His most gracious presence? John Bunyan knew that God was there when he went about tinkering and came to Bedford, and there were three godly women sitting in the sun at work; and as they worked they talked so sweetly that the tinker stood and listened and was drawn to better things. By such means he became a believer and a preacher and the writer of the *Pilgrim's Progress* which has so refreshed us all. The Lord was there, and therefore he dreamed a heavenly dream in Bedford jail. Wherever His people meet, the Lord is graciously near. "Where two or three are gathered together in my name, there am I in the midst of them."

Yes, but *when Christian people go forth to work*, when you come to your Sunday School, or go out with your bundle of tracts to change them on your district, or when

you join a little band and stand in the street corner yonder and lift up your voice in the name of Jesus, you may
expect, if you go with prayer and faith, that it shall be
written, "Jehovah-shammah, the Lord is there." It is only
a young man standing up in a cottage to speak, and he
has not much to say; yet there are penitential tears, and
broken hearts; it is so, for God is there. It is only a humble woman speaking to a few persons of her own class,
and yet angels are rejoicing over a repenting sinner—yes,
because God is there. It is only a little room in one of our
back streets, the neighbors called together, and he is talking of Jesus and His love—oh, but if the Lord be there, do
not tell me that the missionary is not in the apostolic
succession; he need not claim it, he is himself an apostle
of God to those poor people. He wants no gorgeous vest-
ment, nor the swell of organ, nor even the thunders of the
multitude as they raise the solemn hymn. The few so
simple and so poor have God with them, and it is enough.
Wherever you are seeking to do good, in prayerful dependence upon the Holy Spirit, it shall be said "the Lord is
there."

And now, from this time forth, beloved, you that fear
God and think upon His name, *wherever you go*, let it be
said, "Jehovah-shammah, the Lord is there." I often feel
sorry when the Sabbath is nearly over and so do many of
you. I know you wake on Monday morning and take those
shutters down again, or go off to that workshop where
you suffer so much ridicule, or return to the ordinary
grind of daily labor and mix up with so many of the
ungodly; and you do it mournfully. Now, pray that you
may keep up the Sabbath tone all the week. Make every
place, wherever you go, to be the house of God.

A dear brother of ours went to a shop where he worked
with four ungodly men, but his Lord went with him. It
was not long before we had the privilege of baptizing that
friend's master and all his shopmates, for the Lord was
there. The other day there came a fresh man to work who
could not bear to hear a word upon religion, but our brother
was the means of his conversion, and the new man is
coming among us, warm with his first love. Our brother

makes up his mind that he is not to be conquered by any scoffers, but on the contrary he is determined to conquer *them* for Christ. He will not yield to the influences of sin, but he resolves, in the name of the Lord, that evil influences shall yield to the power of truth and to the attractions of the cross. Write across your workshop, "The Lord is here." If you cannot do it literally, do it spiritually, "Jehovah Shammah, the Lord is there."

Do not be found anywhere where you could not say that the Lord was there; but if you are called into the world in the pursuit of your daily vocation, cry unto the Lord, "If thy Spirit go not with me, carry me not up hence." Determine that you will have the Spirit of God with you, and that, be it in a busy city, or be it in the lonesome country while you are hoeing the turnips or attending to a flock of sheep, of every field, and every street, and every room, it shall be said that God is there. Take Jesus with you when you go; and, when you come home, may His Spirit still be with you! God grant that it may be so! The Holy Spirit can work you to this self-same thing.

What shall I say to those who do not know the Lord, and do not care for Him? O friend, the day will come in which Jesus Christ will say to you, "I never knew you: depart from me, ye workers of iniquity." Do not let Him say that; but tonight commence an acquaintance with Him. May His Holy Spirit help you to do so! I am sure the Lord Jesus Christ could not say to me, "I never knew you." It is impossible, because I could reply to Him, "Never knew me, Lord? Why, I have been to Thee with so many burdens, I have run to Thee with so many troubles, that I am sure Thou knowest me as one knows a beggar whom he has relieved many times a day."

> Dost thou ask me who I am?
> Ah, my Lord! thou know'st my name.

Thou rememberest me, for in my despair I cried to thee, and thou didst relieve me of my burden. Thou knowest me, for in my sorrow my broken heart found no comfort but in Thee. Thou hast known me all these years in which I have had to cry to Thee for something to preach about, and for help while preaching. Thou knowest how I have had to come to Thee and confess my failures, and mourn my shortcomings, and lament my sins, and trust in Thy blood for cleansing.

My Lord cannot say that He does not know me, for He has known my soul in adversity. Blessed be His name, I know Him, and lean all my weight upon Him. They that know Him shall be their glory—"Jehovah Shammah, the Lord is there." With Him shall they dwell, world without end. Amen.

NOTES

Jehovah of Hosts—The God of Jacob

George Campbell Morgan (1863-1945) was the son of a British Baptist preacher and preached his first sermon when he was 13 years old. He had no formal training for the ministry, but his tireless devotion to the study of the Bible helped him to become one of the leading Bible teachers of his day. Rejected by the Methodists, he was ordained into the Congregational ministry. He was associated with Dwight L. Moody in the Northfield Bible conferences and as an itinerant Bible teacher. He is best known as the pastor of the Westminster Chapel, London (1904-17 and 1933-45). During his second term there, he had Dr. D. Martyn Lloyd-Jones as his associate.

Morgan published more than 60 books and booklets, and his sermons are found in *The Westminster Pulpit* (London, Pickering and Inglis). This sermon is from Volume 9.

George Campbell Morgan

2

JEHOVAH OF HOSTS— THE GOD OF JACOB

Jehovah of hosts is with us; the God of Jacob is our refuge (Psalm 46:7, 11).

IN THE HISTORY of the human race nothing has ever been done for its help or uplifting save through the principle of faith. Doubt is always destructive. Faith is forever constructive. That is to state the principle in the widest and broadest possible way. I am not now speaking only of the faith of the Christian, though, of course, it is to that I am proposing to come. It is true in every walk of life and every department of thought that the man of faith builds. The man who lacks faith breaks down.

This being granted, I submit that the particular quality of faith which has done most for the uplifting of humanity is that of faith in the living and eternal God. Faith that believes in the existence of God and believes, moreover, in the Divine interest in human affairs is the faith which has most helped the race.

The Fact of God

The fact of God as the foundation of faith is our theme. I am speaking to Christian workers, to those upon whom the burden and the toil that makes His kingdom come is resting, to those who sometimes amid the conflict are weary and almost discouraged. I am perfectly sure that it is the occasional experience of anyone doing real work for God. If we know what it is to get underneath even the edge of the world's agony with the imperial, lonely Christ, then we know what it is to have days of darkness, hours of questionings, problems, trials, temptation, and difficulties in Christian service.

Yet notwithstanding all such hours, and occasions, and

29

questionings, an undercurrent of conviction exists in the heart of every member of the Christian community; it is one of unswerving and unabated confidence in God. He is the rock foundation upon which we build—the strong rock upon which faith fastens while we toil and suffer and serve all the while confident of the ultimate victory.

If I remind you of these things, it is because I think sometimes amid the toil we should stop and be conscious of the rock. The rock is always there, but perhaps the consciousness of some trembling child of God will be stronger for pausing to think of it.

These old Hebrew singers and seers had a very keen consciousness of the fact, though, perchance, they did not understand the nature and character of God as we do. They had to wait for the full shining of light in the Person of Jesus. This Psalm begins with the announcement in a single word of all the truth that it afterward unfolded. God—and the psalmist has said everything when he has said God.

Yet, essential light is always such that we cannot look at it. We have not yet been able to gaze upon pure light. Light must be analyzed to enable us to appreciate it, to understand it. The pure light is the final fact, but the light must be broken up in order that we may apprehend it. After the psalmist has uttered the word which is all conclusive, he proceeds to say things about it until he comes to the seventh verse in the heart of the Psalm, until he comes to the closing sentences of the Psalm, and in these two verses he breaks up for us the essential light. "Jehovah of hosts is with us; the God of Jacob is our refuge." All I want to do is to consider this breaking up of the essential truth concerning God upon which our faith has fastened and must fasten if we are to continue to be workers together with Him and for Him.

Jehovah of Hosts

Will you follow me, then, along two lines of meditation? First, a consideration of the twofold truth about God which my text suggests, and second, the twofold statement the psalmist makes based upon the twofold fact. The twofold fact concerning God—He is Jehovah of hosts, He is the God of Jacob. The twofold declaration he makes about this God; first, "He is with us"; second, "He is our refuge."

First, then, the twofold declaration concerning God: "The Lord of hosts . . . the God of Jacob."

"The Lord of hosts," or, as the American Revision has given it to us, "Jehovah of Hosts," the name by which he knew the Deity as self-existent and eternal. Other names of God which have come to us from the Hebrew people are preceded by qualifying words but never so with Jehovah. The Hebrew never wrote this name fully. It was the unpronounceable name, the incommunicable name, the name that stood lonely in majesty as the sign and symbol of the infinite things of God which no man could perfectly comprehend and therefore no man perfectly explain. Jehovah was the name which most forcefully gave expression to the facts concerning God which were beyond human comprehension—His absoluteness, without beginning, without end, without counsel taken, without forethought—for there was no thought before Him—Jehovah.

If we are wise, we stand with the Jew in the presence of the name and confess our ignorance while we bow in reverential worship. Jehovah speaks of the continuousness of God, the self-determining power of the Most High, and His inward sufficiency, so that there is nothing beyond His consciousness. It is the greatest of all the words into which the fact of God is compressed in such a way as to announce forevermore to men that it cannot be expressed so that the mind of finite man can ever understand it.

The psalmist comes very near qualifying the word for he adds "of hosts." Not that the word "of hosts" really qualifies "Jehovah" for, rather, the word "Jehovah" qualifies the "of hosts."

"Hosts." How is that word used in the Bible? It is employed in the Old Testament Scriptures and in the New Testament in different ways. It is used first with regard to the stars. We read in Genesis, "And the heavens and the earth were finished, and all the host of them" (2:1). In the prophecy of Isaiah, "Lift up your eyes on high, and see

Who hath created these, that bringeth out their host by number; He calleth them all by name; by the greatness of His might, and for that He is strong in power, not one is lacking" (40:26).

The same term is also used of the angels. ". . . I saw the Lord sitting on His throne, and all the host of heaven standing by Him on His right hand and on His left" (1 Kings 22:19); and in the song that sounded o'er Bethlehem's plains after the angel's solo, it is recorded, ". . . there was . . . a multitude of the heavenly host praising God . . ." (Luke 2:13).

In the Book of Exodus the word is applied to the children of Israel. They are spoken of as the host of God. Thus it is used of the stars in the heavens, of the unfallen intelligences that people the world beyond our vision and knowledge, and of the companies of men that march across the earth and dwell upon its surface, of stars and seraphim and saints, host of stars, hosts of angels, hosts of saints. I believe in my text it is used of all these.

This phrase, "Jehovah of hosts," teaches us that Jehovah is absolute, sufficient, and superior. It declares to us that God is the Lord of the heavens and all their inhabitants. As one has beautifully expressed it, "The universe of matter and the world of mind were not only created, but are marshaled and ordered by God." We are now looking upon one side only of the Divine nature and being, thinking of Him as the One Who knows all hosts and marshals and controls them by His own power, and we are reminded of the wisdom of God and of the might and majesty of the Most High—"Jehovah of hosts. . . ."

Turn to the other half of the declaration concerning God. "The God of Jacob. . . ." If we were not so familiar with this text, we should be startled by the very daring of bringing together two such descriptions of God as we have within its compass. "Jehovah of hosts, . . ." and in a moment, by a rapid change of terms, we are given another revelation of God, which I do not hesitate to say is far more startling than the former, especially when considered in the light thereof. "The Lord of hosts, . . ." and then suddenly, "the God of Jacob. . . ." "The Lord of hosts, . . ."

and as the phrase passes our lips we are amid the eternal expanse, the unfallen intelligences, the vision of any one of which would blind us were it granted to us at this moment. And suddenly, almost without warning, we move from the stellar spaces onto the earth. The stars grow dim until they are seen but as flecks and points of glory upon the darkling brow of night; the angels pass from our vision; and we are on one small planet, amid the hosts of heaven, in one small country upon that planet, looking into the face of one lonely man—Jacob. The psalmist says that the God Who is the God of all the hosts is the God of that man as surely and positively interested in that one speck of thinking life as in all the unfallen intelligences of the upper spaces; as surely and as positively committed to that man as to all the order of the infinite universe.

The God of Hosts

We have not yet reached the height and the depth of the mystery. We have not yet reached the word that is most startling of all in this consideration. Notice carefully what the psalmist says: "The God of Jacob. . . ." I think we should not have been quite so startled if the psalmist had said the God of Israel. He says, "the God of Jacob. . . ." I know only one man who is meaner than Jacob and that is Laban. The only comfort I ever got out of Jacob is that he was one too many for Laban. Of all men for astute, hard-driving meanness recommend me to Jacob. But God is "the God of Jacob. . . ." Oh, my soul, here find thy comfort! I do not know whether it helps you, but it helps me. He is the God of Jacob, mean as Jacob was. This is the thing on which my faith fastens. "The Lord of hosts, . . ." yes; but "the God of Jacob! . . ." But was that man such a man as I? The longer I live the more astonished I am that God ever loved me at all. The longer I live the more astonished I am at that infinite grace which found me and loves me and keeps me. The meanness that lurks within, the possibilities of evil that I have discovered make me ask, "Will God look at me?" He is "the God of Jacob." He was his God and loved him notwithstanding all his meanness, enwrapped him with provision, led him, told him where to rest his head, and when he had laid that head upon the stone, linked heaven and earth with a symbolic ladder to teach him His care for him even while he was Jacob. Infinite in His majesty, "The Lord of hosts . . ."; infinite in His mercy, "the God of Jacob. . . ." Stupendous is His power, upholding all things by the Word thereof, "the Lord of hosts . . ."; sublime in His pity, "the God of Jacob. . . ."

This revelation moves me more than any other. The very distance of the other fact enables me to assume an erect posture in the presence of it. "The Lord of hosts . . ."—and I hear the music and rhythm of the eternal order amid stars and angels. "The God of Jacob . . ."—I thought He was far away, I hoped I might, perchance, see the glistening of His dazzling robe of glory among the everlasting spaces. But He is not far away, He is with Jacob! It is not only in immensity but in littleness that God is great. Mark the condescension of this figure of speech; note the beauty of it. Notwithstanding the failure and wreckage of this life, despite the fact that it is anything but what God meant it to be, that in its foolish attempts to create its own destiny and carve its own fortune it has led itself into the region where character is blighted and spoiled by the dwarfing influences of vain ambition, yet the inspiring word comes to me—"the God of Jacob. . . ." He has created man, and man has broken all His laws; but He is his God still and broods over him tenderly, his folly notwithstanding.

Let us consider what the psalmist says concerning these facts. First, then, the declaration, "The Lord of hosts is with us. . . ." May I make application of the truth by reminding you again what this phrase "of hosts" means? He is the God of the stars, the God of the angels, the God of men in multitudes and companies. The God of all these hosts is with us, and for our making, for the making of Jacob, He will press all hosts into service if necessary. "But," you say, "this is imagination. Do you mean to suggest that this God, Who is the God of the individual, of Jacob, will use the stars for our making?" I desire to tell you nothing that is not within the covers of the Bible. I have no commission to speculate or philosophize. I have a commission to preach the Word. Let me read some Old Testament words:

> The kings came and fought,
> Then fought the kings of Canaan,
> In Taanach, by the waters of Megiddo;
> They took no gain of money.
> They fought from heaven,
> The stars in their courses fought against Sisera.
> The river Kishon swept them away,
> That ancient river, the river Kishon. . . .

And then we are not surprised that the writer of the historic fact in poetic language addresses his soul thus: ". . . Oh, my soul, march on with strength." "The Lord of hosts is with us. . . ." The God of the stars in their courses shall fight for me against the foes that hinder me as I climb upward toward the home of God. He will command the whole universe for the making of a soul. Do you doubt me there? Then let me remind you that for the purchase of my soul and yours, for its reconciliation and redemption, He gave in one supreme gift that which was infinitely superior to all the stars—the One by Whose word they were made, and in Whose might they have consisted through the ages. He gave Him for the remaking of my broken, maimed, spoiled life. The stars, the hosts of God if need be, will be pressed into the service of the making of the saint, and into the service of the saint as he goes forth in toil for God.

The Fact of Angels

But what of angels? Need I tarry to say anything about angels? I fear I must. This is a very Sadducean age. I am never quite sure whether there are more Sadducees or Pharisees in the world today. I do not mean in the accidentals of past manifestations but in the essentials. The Pharisee was the ritualist in his age. The Sadducee was the rationalist, and if you want to know the essentials, you can find it in one brief description in your New Testament. ". . . the Sadducees say that there is no resurrection, neither angel, nor spirit. . . ." And there are a great many Sadducees abroad today. They smile and they say, "You do not really believe this story that angels help us."

I believe angels help us. I still believe with the psalmist that "The angel of the Lord encampeth round about them that fear Him. . . ." I still believe with the New Testament writer, "Are they not all ministering spirits, sent forth to do service for the sake of them that shall inherit salvation?" Poetry, do you say? I know it is poetic statement, but it is fact that makes the poetry. I believe that what Jesus said once was true. I do not quite understand it, but I am sure it is true. Jesus said, "See that ye despise not one of these little ones; for I say unto you that in heaven their angels do always behold the face of My Father which is in heaven." I tell you honestly that I do not perfectly understand it. But there are certain things in it I am sure of. "My Father in heaven," the "little ones," and "their angels." How the angel beholds the face of the Father, or how the beholding of the angel saves the child I do not quite know; but I am sure of the Father and sure of the children, and sure of the angels. And men and women, I beseech you, doubt this Sadducean age that questions the ministry of the spirit and the ministries of the angels, and believe me, if we could see things as they are now, the Lord of hosts has His hosts of angels guarding the children, watching our way, preparing as we go.

Angels? The prophet Elisha was shut up in the city, and his servant was terribly anxious, and he said to him, "Master, what shall we do?" And the prophet said to God, "Lord, . . . open his eyes. . . ."

> And lo! to faith's enlightened sight
> All the mountain flamed with light.

Jesus faced His passion, and when a blundering disciple smote His enemy with an old sword, He said: ". . . Put up again thy sword. . . . Thinkest thou that I cannot beseech My Father, and He shall even now send Me more than twelve legions of angels?"

Jehovah with Men

But what about the hosts of men? Is Jehovah indeed with hosts of men? Yes, and not only is He Jehovah of hosts concerning the companies of His saints; Jehovah is the Lord of all hosts and of all the hosts of men. He is the Lord of all the armies in the world. Let no man misunderstand me for a moment. Let me say to you bluntly what is in my deepest soul. I hate all war as I hate hell, and I believe you can never justify it by Christian standards under any circumstances whatever. But if men will fight, God is the God of battles. He does not inspire the battle, but He governs its goings, and remember this, that no army ever marches across any path of this earth but in the check of His strong hand. It may be a little difficult sometimes to understand what God is doing. I suppose there have been moments in the lives of all of us who know anything of what it is to love and serve Him when we have grumbled with Carlyle, "Yes, God is in His heaven, but doing nothing." He is always doing something.

You say, "What has this to do with me?" He will compel the march of men to contribute to the making of men. He will press into the service of turning Jacob into Israel whole armies as they come and go. Hosts of stars, hosts of angels, hosts of men, and the Lord of all of them is with us.

Oh, take heart, my brothers, my sisters! Is the burden pressing heavily, is the toil almost too great to be borne? Do you stand upon the brink of great enterprises, afraid because of the vested interests, because of the hosts of wickedness? I bring you a message full of heart, hope, and courage. God, by His Spirit, sing it as an anthem in your heart. "The Lord of hosts is with us, . . ." and while its music thrills my soul I dare go back to battle and suffering and to the defeat of half an hour because I know at last the victory will be won, and the Lord of hosts cannot be defeated.

God Our Refuge

A final word about the other fact—". . . the God of Jacob is our refuge." What did He do for Jacob? Think of his history. See at what infinite pains God was to make something out of him. Oh, the patience of God! oh, the waiting! oh, the forces pressed into the making of a man! oh, the opened heavens and the ascending and descending angels! oh, the glimpse of hosts He gave him one day! He called the name of one place Mahanaim which means the place of hosts. He said, "With my staff I passed over this Jordan, and now I am become two companies." Jacob, you have to learn that none of them are your own, that the Lord of hosts possesses every last skin of your cattle, and there are other hosts besides. There is Esau's host. He is coming to meet you with armed men. Jacob, you have yet to learn that a man may march against you with armed men all to no purpose if God is on your side; It was in that day that he saw God's host. What he saw, who shall tell? The host of God passed him, and he said, "Mahanaim," it is the place of hosts.

And he went down over the Jabbok, and God met with him and crippled him to make him. It was a wonderful night, only do not let us misinterpret it. I beseech you, do not talk as though Jacob wrestled with God and overcame Him. It is not true. Do not recite Jacob's words in the wrong tone. You know perfectly well that you may say correct words so that the tone gives a lie to the meaning of the words you recite. Do not imagine he said, ". . . I will not let Thee go except Thou bless me." If you want to know all go to the prophecy of Hosea. It is declared he was heard when with strong crying and tears, he said, ". . . I will not let Thee go except Thou bless me." It was a voice choked with sorrow, the voice of a man being beaten, being crippled in the last agony of despair as he went down beneath the pressure of that mysterious hand. He won when he was beaten; he triumphed when he yielded; and God never let him alone until that night by crippling him He broke him.

And the day broke, and the people over the Jabbok saw him coming back again. Let us go and meet him. "Jacob, where have you been?" "Do not call me Jacob. My name is not Jacob. I was Jacob, a mere supplanter; but I am Israel, God-governed. Do not call me Jacob any more." I think

I would have said, "Man, tell me, what is the matter? When I saw you last night, dividing up those bands to mollify Esau, you were erect, but now you are lame." "That limp will follow me to the end. It is the patent of my nobility; it is evidence of the fact that God has won at last." ". . . the God of Jacob is our refuge."

Oh, man, conscious of your own weakness! Oh, brother, conscious of the evil within you, which baffles, beats and spoils you, ". . . the God of Jacob is our refuge." When the only pillow we have is a stone—a hard, unkind, unsympathetic stone—then will He open His heaven, so that His hosts may teach us that they with us are more than they that be against us; and if the God of Jacob be our refuge He will put His hands upon us, and, it may be, wound us, but the wounding is only for the deeper healing; it may be, cripple us, but the crippling is only for the stronger work that lies beyond; it may be, shatter all our cherished dreams, smiting the light of the mirage into nothingness; but it is in order that He may light the truer light and give to us the very nature of the sons of God.

I do not think any of us become Israels until we have been at the Jabbok. We never get to power until His hands have been upon us, and sometimes today as in the dim and distant past, God has to put the scar on the flesh and crippling on the life before He can do very much with us. Oh, dear heart, tried, as by fire, sing while the fire burns, sing while the pain is hot. If you are trusting Him, He breaks to make, He cripples to crown. Then by God's grace we are going on; we are not thinking of resigning; we are not going to give this fight up, or anything up, except sin. "The Lord of hosts, . . ." marshaling all for our making, ". . . is with us; the God of Jacob, . . ." patient and strong and purposeful, ". . . is our refuge." We will follow, we will trust, we will fight—God helping us.

". . . the God of Jacob is our refuge." Another word will convey the true meaning of this. The God of Jacob is "our high place"; "The name of the Lord is a strong tower, The righteous runneth into it and is set on high (and is safe)." Such is the real word: The God of Jacob is "our high place." What means it? We have come down from immensity to localized position, from hosts to individuality, from the magnificent outlook of the Divine movements to personal life. And what is the promise about the God of Jacob? That He will be our "high place"; that we may be set in Him above circumstances, above enemies, above self, and so we look to the future with all confidence and security, because "The Lord of hosts is with us; the God of Jacob is our refuge."

If this announcement engender within us confidence, rest, assurance, it must also produce consecration. If looking on at our work with its light and its possibilities of sorrow and joy, we are confident and glad and the tone of our voice has in it the ring of the triumphant hosanna, if we are confident by reason of these words, then let it be remembered they must also produce consecration.

How will the fact of the Divine presence be manifested to the world? By the effect it produces upon us. So, while we take our joy and comfort out of the blessed thought that "the Lord of hosts is with us, . . ." we must not forget that the eyes of men are fixed upon us to discover Him of Whom we speak, and they will not see Him in shining glory; but if "the Lord of hosts is with us," and "the God of Jacob is our refuge," in the quiet calm of our spirit, in the tenderness of our love, in the straightness of our dealings with each other, in all the growing beauty of our lives, men will see that the Lord of hosts—of order, of precision, and magnificence—and the God of Jacob—of love, of care, and sympathy—is with us. Ours is the blessing, but ours is also the responsibility. Let us remember that the effects produced will be in proportion to our realization of the Divine presence, and our realization of the Divine presence will be in proportion to our yielding of ourselves to the will that is known, to the word that is spoken, that doing the will we may know the doctrine and may pass from glory into glory, the light and beauty of the Divine shining evermore upon our faces, and in our lives, that others, too, may come to see the glory of the Lord of hosts, the patience of the God of Jacob.

NOTES

The Cry of the Orphaned Heart

John Ker (1819-1886) is little known today, but in his
day he was a respected preacher and professor of preaching and pastoral work at the United Free Church Semi-
nary in Glasgow, Scotland.

He published two volumes of sermons: this one is from
the *Sermons Second Series,* published in Edinburgh in
1888 by David Douglas.

John Ker

3

THE CRY OF THE ORPHANED HEART

Doubtless Thou art our Father (Isaiah 63:10).

IF THIS CHAPTER is read, it will be seen that these words came from the heart of the Jewish people when they felt themselves "aliens from the commonwealth of Israel, and strangers to the covenants of promise." They had wandered from the God of their fathers, and they feel as if their fathers had cast them off. If Abraham were to appear on earth, he would not know them; if Jacob were to return, he would not acknowledge them; and what then can they do? They cannot endure life, cannot bear the burden of its sorrows and struggles without a father and a friend. What can they do but pass up beyond men and seek a father in God? Their heart is an orphan everywhere else and is forced to this door of refuge—"Doubtless Thou—Thou art our Father." It is thousands of years since this cry was uttered, but it has never died out, and it is present still in many a spirit. Let us listen to it and think of some of the things which it suggests.

A Deep Longing of the Human Heart

1. The words express *a deep longing of the human heart.* With all its folly and frivolity and sin, the heart of man has been made to feel after these words: "Our Father— our Father which art in heaven." The lower creatures have not this cry because they have not our wants, our aspirations, or the possibility of our hopes. God opens His hand and casts down their food, and they look down for it; but there is something within man's heart which bids him look up and see God's hand and seek from it something higher. "Your heavenly Father feedeth them"; their Provider is your Father. There are wonderful instincts among them—most wonderful often in the most minute.

43

The bees and ants have their policy, their regulated industry, we might almost say their civilization. But what curious microscope ever discovered among them a spire pointing heavenward or tokens of prayer and praise? The magnet which is passed over the earth to draw things upward finds nothing in this world which trembles and turns to it save the human heart. It is very true that many hearts make little visible response and seem to bear the want of a heavenly Father very lightly. But even in them there may be discerned the heart-hunger that shows itself in unnatural cravings which the lower creatures do not feel. The void may be discovered in the restless attempts men make to fill it. It is true also that there are times when the evil fumes of material sin deaden the hearts of men of whom we could wish better things. But, when we look at the length and breadth of man's history, it tells us that this cry constantly returns, sometimes exceedingly great and bitter, sometimes sinking to a low moan or a suppressed whisper, "O that I knew where I might find Him!" There have been men in all ages to whom the answer of this cry has been the one necessity of life, and if you could convince them that it is impossible to find a heavenly Father they would smile no more. Good were it for us, good for all of us, that we had never been born. Better never enter the world than find it a world without God and without hope.

Difficult to Speak These Words with Full Assurance

2. And yet it is often *difficult to speak these words with full assurance.* The struggle to reach them is evident in the men who use them here and is felt in the very word "doubtless," with which they begin their claim. When a man says, "Surely, surely, it must be so," he shows how hard it has been for him to make the truth his own. We may appeal to many still if it is not so. You will say, "I long for it, I will not give up the hope of reaching it—no, not for all the world. I think I can sometimes look up and truly say it; but to have it as a clear and constant possession of the soul, this is very difficult. Would that I had

always a cloudless spiritual sky above me when I look to God! Doubtless Thou art our Father."

It would take long to number up all the difficulties, but we shall mention some. There is one, which belongs specially to our time, in the *mind* of man as it deals with the universe and its laws. There is a form of science which says, "I have ranged the world, and there is nothing in it but material law, iron links riveted, each to each, so fast that prayer can never pass up through them, or the hand of a heavenly Helper come down. I sound the depths, I scale the heights, and there is no door or window, not a chink or eyelet-opening through which a Father can be seen. There may be a heart in man, but there is no heart beyond to answer it; or, if there be, the heart of man can never reach it." Let us thank God that it is not all science, nor the clearest-eyed, that speaks thus; but the voice is loud enough to fill some with fear.

And, besides the mind, the *heart* finds difficulties in itself. There are so many things in life which make it hard to believe in the love of God. There are the losses and crosses, sore bereavements, terrible agonies of doubt and spiritual darkness, from which God could surely keep us free. We say with the man in the gospels. "Lord, if Thou wilt, Thou canst." It is not want of power; is it then want of will? Can it be true that "like as a father pitieth his children, so the Lord pitieth them that fear Him"? It is easy, very easy, when the sea is smooth, and the ship in full sail, to talk in a general way of the Fatherhood of God; but when gulfs are yawning, and cries of drowning men are around, and deep answers to deep in our own soul, then to say, "Thou art our Father," does not come so readily to the lip.

And still beyond the mind and heart there is the *conscience*. When we think of a Father in heaven, we must think of a righteous Father, of one "who is of purer eyes than to behold iniquity." The weak, indulgent fatherhood, which is passed so lightly from hand to hand, will not fit into the parts of the world's history which show the terrible penalties of sin; it will not satisfy the soul when it is brought face to face with the majesty of God's law and the holiness of His character. When I look within, I may please myself in comparisons with others, or in little complacencies of my own temperament; but should the Spirit of God lead me into His presence, can I help feeling how I have defaced His image and given over to the vainest and basest things the love which belonged to Him alone—how I have dethroned Him from His place and put up too often the most unworthy idols in His room? It would be very ill for us if we could take all this with a light heart and imagine that if we frame our mouth to the word "Father," it will cover all. The conscience, when stirred, forces a man to a harder struggle.

A Feeling Which Can Be and Has Been Reached

3. But, with all these difficulties, it is *a feeling which can be and has been reached.* Yes, it can be reached. We could never believe that such a deep longing had been implanted in man to be forever unanswered—a cry pressed from his heart to be mocked with endless disappointment. If a man cannot trust in a God for this, he might in some ways find hope in the structure of the universe and infer that the most profound cry of the heart shall have something to meet it. And it has been reached. In view of all the difficulties of mind and heart and conscience, there have been men who could look up and say, "Doubtless Thou art our Father." They have said it not only in sunshine but in storm and in the shadow of death; have given up their lives that they might testify to it clearly and fearlessly; and have shut the door, and said it to their Father who seeth in secret, that they might not seek the praise of men. Those who have been able to say it in times past have been more than the stars of the sky for multitude, and let us bless God they are round us yet in duty and trial, in the world's work, and on solitary sickbeds, doing their Father's will and bearing it.

But we are here to think of One, the greatest of all. Even those who take the lowest view of Jesus Christ will admit that He, beyond all others, taught men to think of God as a Father and gave the example of it in His own life and death. How strong it made Him, and how patient, how active in doing good, how comforted in solitude, that His Father had sent Him, and was present with Him, putting the cup of suffering into His hand, and ready to receive Him when He said, "Father, into thy hands I commend my spirit!" But His example, His influence, wonderful as they are, would not enable us to follow Him to God as a Father unless there was something in His death which laid hold of us with stronger power. It behooved Him to be made like unto His brethren, to make reconciliation for the sins of the people. He drank the cup we deserved to drink that He might put into our hand a cup of blessing. "This cup is the new covenant in my blood, shed for many for the remission of sins." It is this which enables us to go to God the Judge of all with confidence because we go through the blood of sprinkling. In the storm of soul which an awakened conscience rouses, this is the anchor which holds—not my character or repentance or the new life formed in me by Christ for these still remain imperfect; I need a perfect righteousness to meet a perfect law, and I can find it only when I am found in Him.

Here the conscience may have rest for all the guilty past that it may begin its new service of love to the God and Father of our Lord and Savior Jesus Christ. And when the conscience can say, My Father! the heart begins to say it also. "He that spared not His own Son, but delivered Him up for us all, how shall He not with Him also freely give us all things?" New comforts and hopes come down into the soul like the angel that came into the agony of the garden to strengthen Christ Himself—nay, Christ Himself returns, as He said, "I will not leave you orphans: I will come to you." And then, when the heart finds a Father in God, the difficulties of the mind about the laws of nature disappear.

These laws are but the expression of His will always and everywhere. Every blossom, ay, and every blight, every sunbeam and every cloud, are in His hand for good to me if I love Him. It needs no door or window, no chink or eyelet-opening through which we may communicate for all the earth and sky are transparent, and material laws are not impenetrable armor laid on nature but are "touched and turned to finest air." When the heart has found a Father in God, all the world's laws cannot lay hands on it to imprison it; it moves "through the midst of them, and so passes by."

Not Generally Gained at Once

4. But this full sense of God's Fatherhood is *not generally gained at once*. We do not say that the position is not gained at once. As soon as any one comes to God through Christ, he is no more a stranger and an enemy but a child, and all the dealings of God with him are paternal dealings. But he may fail to recognize a Father's voice and hand. When his conscience comes under the shadow of guilt, he says, "I am no more worthy to be called thy son, make me as one of thy hired servants; I would be in the house, but I cannot be in the family." Or, when his heart is sick and sore with loss and pain, he says, "Surely against me is He turned; He turneth His hand against me all the day." Or God seems so far away, shut out by heavens of iron, that he cannot reach Him. "Also when I cry and shout, He shutteth out my prayer." All this has been felt, is felt now, most of all by those who desire to have God not as a name but as a living God and Father.

Is it so, then, that you feel yourself in this state and that you wish to rise from it to a more clear and assured use of the words, "Doubtless Thou art our Father"? Then think of these ways by which it may be gained. Come, first of all, by a more simple and loving faith to the death of Christ in the fullness of its meaning. Bring all sin and shortcoming, and acquaint yourself with God through Him, and be at peace. He will take you by the hand and lead you to Him who is reconciling sinners to Himself, "not imputing unto them their trespasses." And then, if you would retain it, seek more fully to give Christ entrance into your heart and life. He Himself has said, "If a man love Me, he will keep my words: and my Father will love him, and we will come unto him, and make our abode with him."

Whether He comes with a word of active duty or a

word of patient suffering, let us take it and put it into our heart, and we shall find before long God's fatherly kindness in it. As the heart is purified, we see God. And that we may have power for this, we must realize more constantly the presence of Christ's Holy Spirit. It is He who leads us to be Christ's guests in His house, and brings Christ to be a guest in ours, and conveys to the soul at last the full sense of sonship. To have God for our Father is not merely to be forgiven, it is not even to be sanctified; it is to be one with Him as one speaks with a friend. It is peculiarly the work of the Holy Spirit to lead us into this inmost sanctuary of sonship. "As many as are led by the Spirit of God, they are the sons of God." But to be led by Him, we must not grieve Him by sin or neglect but welcome His whispered admonitions; and then, as we listen and obey, we shall reach the innermost room where "the Spirit beareth witness with our spirit, that we are the children of God."

There are three chambers, then, by which we advance to the assurance of Fatherhood in God. The first is the upper chamber of Jerusalem which comes to us ever and again in the Lord's table with its offer of pardon and peace. The second is the chamber of the heart to which we give Him admission in love and obedience. And the third is the home where the Holy Spirit teaches us to cry, "Abba, Father." Every Christian should know something of all of them at first; some reach an intimate knowledge of them very soon; but in general the progress is gradual from the peace of forgiveness to the house where we can say, "Doubtless Thou art our Father," with an entire conviction which fills the heart and the life.

A Matter of Infinite Moment to Us All

5. We say, last, that to use these words truly is *a matter of infinite moment to us all*. Here is a friend we need in every stage of life and in every event of it. It comes with its invitation to the young: "Wilt thou not from this time cry unto Me, My Father, Thou art the guide of my youth?" In years long ago, when the world was in its spring-time, the voice of the Lord God was heard in the

garden, and it is this way still. The world is not safe or truly happy without His guidance.

> Now seek Him: in his favor life is found,
> All bliss beside a shadow or a sound.

And when the world seems growing old to us, and the autumn leaves are falling, and the woods are bare, and we look up straight into the sky, it is cheerless if the face of a Father does not meet us there, who knoweth our frame and remembereth that we are dust. And if there be some young man who has wandered far from his true home, it will never be well with him till he comes to himself and says, "I will arise and go to my Father!" Or if there be some who in the world's work have despised the better portion, it is time to come with the prayer, "Bless me, even me also, O my Father!"—while they can recover the birthright and the full inheritance of the elder-born. Whatever our estate in life may be, it will find what it needs in this name if we can truly use it. The cup of happiness will be sweeter when a Father's hand provides it, our sorrows soothed when He pours in comfort, our burdens lighter when He sustains declining years, not lonely when God says to old age, "I am He"; and death will not be dark with the promise, "If children, then heirs; heirs of God, and joint-heirs with Christ."

It is in Jesus Christ that all the promises of God are "Yea and Amen"; and in the memorials of His death and sacrifice He is willing to certify and seal them to us if we draw near in faith. Let us listen as He speaks of a Father's love of heart: "Therefore doth my Father love Me, because I lay down my life." "As the Father hath loved Me, so have I loved you: continue ye in my love." And then, as He leaves, He points to heaven and says, "I ascend unto my Father, and your Father: and to my God, and your God." Coming down to our level that He may attract us, He thus raises us to His, that we may look away to the infinite and endless hope, "Father, I will that they also, whom Thou hast given Me, be with Me where I am, that they may behold my glory: for Thou lovedst Me before the foundation of the world." If we could only take one of these words, we who were far off might come nigh and claim God by the name which will make life happy, death hopeful, and eternity safe—"Doubtless Thou art our Father, though Abraham be ignorant of us, and Israel acknowledge us not: Thou, O Lord, art our Father, our Redeemer: thy name is from everlasting."

The God of the Patriarchs

George H. Morrison (1866-1928) assisted the great Alexander Whyte in Edinburgh, pastored two churches, and then became pastor in 1902 of the distinguished Wellington Church on University Avenue in Glasgow. His preaching drew great crowds; in fact, people had to line up an hour before the services to be sure to get seats in the large auditorium. Morrison was a master of imagination in preaching, yet his messages are solidly biblical. From his many published volumes of sermons, this message, found in *The Weaving of Glory,* was published by Hodder and Stoughton, London.

George H. Morrison

4

THE GOD OF THE PATRIARCHS

The God of Abraham, and the God of Isaac, and the God of Jacob (Acts 7:32).

THERE IS NO knowledge attainable by man so vital as the knowledge of his God. To know Him with whom we have to do is the most important thing in human life. When we remember that without His hand not a blade of grass would have been green—when we remember that we depend on Him for every heartbeat and for every breath—when we remember that time is but an island engirdled by the ocean of eternity, who does not feel the pressure to know God? If life eternal be life in glorious fullness, then to God must be eternal life. Did we know God in all His height and depth, we should have conquered time and death forevermore. And that is why, in this strange life of ours, with all its struggling interests and ambitions, there is nothing that can for a moment be compared with knowing Him with whom we have to do.

Far more important than attaining wealth, though that be the one passion of the market—far more important than achieving fame, that last infirmity of noble mind—far more important than anything on earth, in present influence and in eternal issue, is knowing whose we are and whom we serve. Now that is the value of such texts as this. They illuminate the character of God. They draw aside, if only by a little, the cloudy curtain that conceals the throne. And so tonight I would dwell upon this text for it has given me a threefold glimpse of God, and what in quiet hours it has given me, it is my duty and my joy to give to you.

The first truth I learn from our text is this, that

God Is the God of Separate Individuals

When we go back in thought to those dim days that

lie upon the farthest verge of history, we are oppressed, wherever we may turn, by a strange feeling as of shadowy multitude. We catch the confused sound of human voices as in a distant murmuring of ocean; we come on traces of unnumbered hordes moving across the world like tidal waters; we light on relics of pyramid or fort where thousands must have ingloriously toiled, and of battles where thousands must have fallen, and some, it may be, gloriously died. Always, in that dim and distant past, the feeling of multitude is overwhelming. Always there are confused and shadowy masses till the sense of the individual is lost. And it is then, over that boundless welter—above that rocking and surging of humanity— that there rings out from the eternal throne, "I am the God of Abraham, of Isaac, and of Jacob." He is not only the God of the innumerable; He is the God of the individual soul. Where you and I hear but a distant murmuring, He hears the separate beat of every heart.

Viewed from the standpoint of the twentieth century, there is nought visible save shadowy multitude; but viewed from the altitude of heaven, the one is as conspicuous as the all. Not only was God guiding those migrations which moved in a wisdom higher than their own. Not only, as on primeval chaos, was there the brooding of the Holy Spirit. Every hand had its distinctive touch, and every lip had its peculiar cry, and every heart had its own separate burden for the God of Abraham, of Isaac, and of Jacob.

Indeed, that is one great distinction between natural and revealed religion for the one thing that natural religion cannot do is to assure us of the individual care of God. The god of natural religion, as it seems to me, is like the driver of some eastern caravan, and he drives his caravan, with skill unerring, over the desert to the gleaming city. But he never halts for any bruised mortal, nor waits to minister to any dying woman, nor even for a moment checks his team to ease the agonies of any child. That is the god of natural religion—the mighty tendency that makes for righteousness. Imperially careful of the whole, he is sovereignly careless of the one.

And over against that god, so dark and terrible, there stands forever the God of revelation, saying in infinite and individual mercy, "I am the God of Abraham, of Isaac, and of Jacob." He, too, is making for a city which hath foundations and whose streets are golden. But He hath an ear for every feeble cry, and a great compassion for every bruised heart, and a watchful pity, like a mother's pity, for lips that are craving for a little water. It was a great thought which Peter uttered when he said to all who read, "He careth for you." But Paul was nearer the heart of the eternal when he said, "He loved me, and gave Himself for me."

This thought of God, as I need hardly tell you, is countersigned in the clearest way by Christ. The God of Christ, in communistic ages, is the asylum of individuality. It is true that there was something in a crowd that stirred our Savior to His depths. He was moved with compassion when He saw the multitude as a flock of sheep without a shepherd. And when He came over against the city of Jerusalem where the murmur of life was and where the streets were thronged, looking, He was intensely moved and wept. There was a place for the all within that heart of His. He saw life steadily and saw it whole. There was not a problem of these teeming multitudes but had its last solution in His blood.

Yet He who thus encompassed the totality in a love that was majestic to redeem, had a heart that never for an instant faltered in its passionate devotion to the one. Living for mankind, He spoke His deepest when His whole audience was one listener. Dying for mankind, His heart was thrilled with the agonized entreaty of one thief. For one coin the woman swept the house; for one sheep the shepherd faced the midnight; for one son, and him a sorry prodigal, the father in the home was brokenhearted. My brother, that is complete assurance that our God is the God of individuals. You are as much His care as if no other man nor angel moved in heaven or earth. He is Almighty and takes the whole wide universe into the covering hollow of His hand, yet He is the God of Abraham, of Isaac, and of Jacob.

The second truth I learn from our text is this, that

God Is the God of Differing Personalities

As the three figures mentioned in our text move silently across the page of Scripture, one of the first things to impress us in them is the distinctness of their personalities. I have seen sometimes in an old Scottish home a series of pictures of the family ancestors. I have no doubt these ancestors existed in the warm imagination of the artist. But what has often struck me in these pictures is not the differences of face and form but the extraordinary and unearthly likeness among these elegant tokens of gentility. Now if the picture-gallery of God were such a fiction, I should expect to find a sameness of that kind. I should expect to find these ancestors of Israel painted, as it were, with common lines. And to me it is a kind of quiet assurance that I am dealing in the Word with real men when I discover in the remotest of them a personality that could never be mistaken. You never could confuse one with the other. They are as different in tone and temper as is the twilight from the dawn. And yet that God who is the God of one is not less really God of the other two—the God of Abraham, of Isaac, and of Jacob.

Think for a moment of these three personalities, that you may understand the grandeur of our text.

First you have Abraham, the man of faith and of the splendid heroism which faith inspires—the man to whom the call of God is everything and who is never disobedient to that call—the man who sees with an inspired directness, who dares with the fine audacity of greatness, who never rears his tent against the storm but close beside his tent he builds an altar. Here is a man who always must be great, gifted with all capacity for leadership, cleaving his way through a thousand lesser things to grasp and grip the things that really matter, a man as large of heart as he is tender, and of a certain sweet and beautiful simplicity—such is the personality of Abraham.

And then you have Isaac, meditative Isaac—Isaac who went out into the fields to meditate at evening—Isaac who was never born to greatness, but only had greatness thrust upon him. A man not fitted for the strenuous life but rather for the quiet and retired life—a lover of the sanctities of home and of the sweet serenities of nature—a quiet believer in his father's God though endowed with nothing of his father's heroism, not ardent, not intense, and never masterful. Love divine meant much to Isaac, but the warmth of human love meant even more; a man domesticated, and in love with peace, and hating strife, and with a tinge of melancholy—such is the personality of Isaac.

And then lastly you have Jacob, different from Isaac as night is from day, a man of power in every line of him, who would have been a millionaire but for the grace of God. Shrewd, subtle, infinitely capable, not gifted at his birth with scrupulosity, a man whom the devil could have used magnificently had not God in His preventing mercy been beforehand; a man with that splendid genius for commerce that has been the birthmark of his Hebrew race, yet never lacking that other Hebrew birthmark, the awful sense of an Almighty God. In every sense of the word a strong man—a man who knew what he wanted and would have it—a man who was not to be baffled in his quest, whether his quest was a bargain or a woman—a man who could spring as swiftly as a tiger and yet like a tiger could lie still and wait—such is the personality of Jacob.

The God of Abraham, of Isaac, and of Jacob—do you see the glorious compass of that now? Separate as the east is from the west, each found his rest and his reward in Him. So do I learn that the God of revelation has a heart that is bigger than our widest difference and has room in His love, and in His service too, for men who stand apart as night from day.

This feature, too, of the divine character is clearly exhibited by Jesus Christ. His God appeals not to one type of man; His God appeals to all. There are certain theologies which so exhibit God as to make Him the possession of a party. The God of Calvinism, for instance, was so stern that one who was not stern was apt to be repelled. But this is the wonder of the God of Jesus, that He has a message for a thousand hearts and kindles into love and ministry every variety of personality. He is the God of Peter with his fine impetuousness and of John with his perfect genius for loving; of Thomas with his brooding melancholy and of Paul with his enthusiastic ardor. He is the God of Martha in her restlessness and in all her bustling and womanly activity; but not less truly is He the God of Mary, whose eyes are homes of silent prayer. That is why, when God in Christ is preached, you shall have every type within the congregation. That is why the mother in the home may pray with confidence for all her children. She is not praying to the God of Abraham only, though even that would be a glorious privilege. She prays to the God of Abraham, of Isaac, and of Jacob.

Then the third truth I learn from our text is this, that

God Is the God of Succeeding Generations

Abraham and Isaac and Jacob were not only men of differing personality—you must not forget that they were also men of separate and succeeding generations. They were not brothers as Cain and Abel were. They were not contemporaries like John and Peter. They did not live under a common roof nor share in the fond affection of one mother. One grew to manhood as the other aged, and took the torch out of a dying hand, and held it aloft that it might guide the pilgrims when the last bearer was sleeping in his grave.

Now in history there have been generations that differed but little from those preceding them. The same sun has shone upon the children that fell with beauty upon the fathers' world. But if you have ever studied the book of Genesis (and there is no book more worthy to be studied), you will have found that that does not apply to the generations of the patriarchs. The battles which Isaac had to fight were not the battles which Abraham had to fight. The difficulties which tried the powers of Jacob were not the difficulties which had confronted Isaac. Each of them had his own task that he must do, and his own victory that he must win, and his own trial that he must meet and master if he was ever to hear the triumph-song. There was a different environment for each of them; there was a differing outlook on the world. Time moved, and moving brought its changes, and of these changes the children were the heirs. So Jacob woke, and the world that met his eyes was not the world that Isaac had delighted in, nor was the world of Isaac that of Abraham.

My brother, when you reflect on that, does it not illuminate our text? God is the God of succeeding generations—of Abraham, of Isaac, and of Jacob. No generation can exhaust His name. No single age can know Him in His fullness. Not even Abraham, for all his faith, can learn the largeness of the heart of God. There is something left for Isaac to discover as he meditates in the fields at eventide, and when Isaac has been gathered to his fathers, still is there fresh light to flash on Jacob. No age has a monopoly of God. None must dictate to the coming days. Even an Abraham, for all his faith, only knows in part and sees in part. Abraham shall sleep, and Isaac shall awake, and Isaac dying shall give place to Jacob, and that one God who was the God of Abraham shall be the God of succeeding generations.

One might have thought that in a new environment there would have been needed for mankind a new divinity. When knowledge had widened, and all the world was different, would not the heart demand a different God? My brother, this is the strange thing of it, that though everything changes as generations pass, the heart still needs, with an undying need, the God who spoke to men so long ago. Isaac hungers for the eternal Being, and finding Him, He is the God of Abraham. Jacob dreams, and dreaming, sees the throne, and on the throne there sits the God of Isaac. He is the God of succeeding generations.

And so tonight, facing our work again, you and I will take comfort in our God. We shall not be cowards when new truth is uttered for He is the God of succeeding generations. Our fathers trusted in Him and were not ashamed, and now in our new world we need Him still. Still do we hunger, though everything is altered, for Him who was our fathers' God. And when our task is over, and we sleep, and our children are carrying on the warfare, still, though heaven and earth have passed away, the God of Isaac will be the God of Jacob. It is only in that faith we can be hopeful. It is only in that faith we can be true. It is only in that faith that we can welcome every discovery which science brings.

Let there be light, although the light should penetrate many a secret that seemed big with heaven—He is the God of succeeding generations. My brother, we know not what is coming on the world, and we see not the mighty changes yet to be. Dimly we feel that those who are now children will live and battle in an altered universe. But we know that whatever change may come, the human heart will still break through to God, and finding Him who is their deepest need, will find He is the God of long ago. Were He the God of Abraham alone, then all the glory would be in bygone days. Were He the God of Isaac only, then I should have no hope but for tonight. But I look backward with adoring gratitude, and I look forward with a heart of rest, when I remember that the God I trust is the God of Abraham, of Isaac, and of Jacob.

NOTES

The Shepherd—The Stone of Israel

Alexander MacLaren (1826-1910) was one of Great Britain's most famous preachers. While pastoring the Union Chapel, Manchester (1858-1903), he became known as "the prince of expository preachers." Rarely active in denominational or civic affairs, MacLaren invested his time in studying the Word in the original and sharing its truths with others in sermons that are still models of effective expository preaching. He published a number of books of sermons and climaxed his ministry by publishing his monumental *Expositions of Holy Scripture*.

This message is taken from *Week-Day Evening Addresses*, published by Funk and Wagnalls Company (1902).

Alexander MacLaren

5

THE SHEPHERD—THE STONE OF ISRAEL

The Mighty God of Jacob. From thence *is* the Shepherd, the stone of Israel (Genesis 49:24).

A SLIGHT alteration in the rendering will probably bring out the meaning of these words more correctly. The last two clauses should perhaps not be read as a separate sentence. Striking out the supplement "is," and letting the previous sentence run on to the end of the verse, we get a series of names of God, in apposition with each other, as the sources of the strength promised to the arms of the hands of the warlike sons of Joseph. From the hands of the mighty God of Jacob—from thence, from the Shepherd, the stone of Israel—the power will come for conflict and for conquest. This exuberant heaping together of names of God is the mark of the flash of rapturous confidence which lit up the dying man's thoughts when he turned to God.

When he begins to think of Him he cannot stay his tongue. So many aspects of His character, so many remembrances of His deeds come crowding into his mind; so familiar and so dear are they that he must linger over the words and strive by this triple repetition to express the manifold preciousness of Him whom no name, nor crowd of names, can rightly praise. So earthly love ever does with its earthly objects, inventing and reiterating epithets which are caresses. Such repetitions are not tautologies for each utters some new aspect of the one subject and comes from a new gush of heart's love toward it. And something of the same rapture and unwearied recurrence to the Name that is above every name should mark the communion of devout souls with their heavenly Love.

What a wonderful burst of such praise flowed out from

David's thankful heart in his day of deliverance like some strong current with its sevenfold wave, each crested with the Name! "The Lord is my rock, and my fortress, and my deliverer: my God, my strength, in whom I will trust; my buckler, and the horn of my salvation, and my high tower."

These three names which we find here are striking and beautiful in themselves, in their juxtaposition, in their use on Jacob's lips. They seem to have been all coined by him for, if we accept this song as a true prophecy uttered by him, we have here the earliest instance of their occurrence. They have all a history and appear again expanded and deepened in the subsequent Revelation. Let us look at them as they stand.

1. The Mighty God of Jacob

The meaning of such a name is clear enough. It is He who has shown Himself mighty and mine by His deeds for me all through my life. The dying man's thoughts are busy with all that past from the day when he went forth from the tent of Isaac and took of the stones of the field for his pillow when the sun went down. A perplexed history it had been with many a bitter sorrow and many a yet bitterer sin. Passionate grief and despairing murmurs he had felt and flung out while it slowly unfolded itself. When the Pharaoh had asked, "How old art thou?" he had answered in words which owe their somberness partly to obsequious assumption of insignificance in such a presence, but have a strong tinge of genuine sadness in them too: "Few and evil have the days of the years of my life been." But lying dying there with it all well behind him, he has become wiser; and now it looks to him as one long showing forth of the might of his God who had been with him all his life long and had redeemed him from all evil. He has got far enough away to see the lie of the land as he could not do while he was toiling along the road. The barren rocks and white snow glow with purple as the setting sun touches them. The struggles with Laban; the fear of Esau; the weary work of toilsome years; the sad day when Rachel died and left him the "son of her sorrow"; the heart sickness of the long years of Joseph's loss—all have faded away or been changed into thankful wonder at God's guidance. The one thought which the dying man carries out of life with him is: God has shown Himself mighty, and He has shown Himself mine.

For each of us, our own experience should be a revelation of God. The things about Him which we read in the Bible are never living and real to us till we have verified them in the facts of our own history. Many a word lies on the page or in our memories, fully believed and utterly shadowy until in some soul's conflict we have had to grasp it and found it true. Only so much of our creed as we have proved in life is really ours. If we will only open our eyes and reflect upon our history as it passes before us, we shall find every corner of it filled with the manifestations to our hearts and to our minds of a present God. But our folly, our stupidity, our impatience, our absorption with the mere outsides of things, our self-will blind us to the Angel with the drawn sword who resists us as well as to the Angel with the lily who would lead us. So we waste our days, are deaf to His voice speaking through all the clatter of tongues, and are blind to His bright presence shining through all the dimness of earth; and, for far too many of us, we never can see God in the present but only discern Him when He has passed by like Moses from his cleft. Like this same Jacob, we have to say: "Surely God was in this place, and I knew it not." Hence we miss the educational worth of our lives; are tortured with needless cares; are beaten by the poorest adversaries; and grope amid what seems to us a chaos of pathless perplexities when we might be marching on assured and strong with God for our guide and the hands of the Mighty One of Jacob for our defense.

Notice, too, how distinctly the thought comes out in this name—that the very vital center of a man's religion is his conviction that God is his. He will not be content with thinking of God as the God of his fathers; he will not even be content with associating himself with them in the common possession; but he must feel the full force of the intensely personal bond that knits him to God and God to him. Of course such a feeling does not ignore the blessed fellowship and family who also are held in this bond. The God of Jacob is to the patriarch also the God of Abraham, and of Isaac, and of Jacob. But that comes second, and this comes first. Each man for himself must put forth the hand of his own faith and grasp that great hand for his own guide. "*My* Lord and *my* God" is the true form of the confession. "He loved *me* and gave Himself for *me*" is the shape in which the Gospel of Christ melts the soul. God is mine because His love individualizes me, and I have a distinct place in His heart, His purposes, and His deeds. God is mine because by my own individual act—the most personal which I can perform—I cast myself on Him; by my faith I appropriate the common salvation and open my being to the inflow of His power. God is mine, and I am His in that wonderful mutual possession with perpetual interchange of giving and receiving not only gifts but selves which makes the very life of love, whether it be love on earth or love in heaven.

Remember, too, the profound use which our Lord made of this name wherein the man claims to possess God. Because Moses at the bush called God the God of Abraham, and of Isaac, and of Jacob, they cannot have ceased to be. The personal relations which subsist between God and the soul that clasps Him for its own demand an immortal life for their adequate expression and make it impossible that death's skeleton fingers should have power to untie such a bond. Anything is conceivable rather than that the soul which can say "God is mine" should perish. And that continued existence demands, too, a state of being which shall correspond to itself in which its powers shall all be exercised, its desires fulfilled, its possibilities made facts. Therefore there must be "the resurrection." "God is not ashamed to be called their God, for He hath prepared for them a city."

The dying patriarch left to his descendants the legacy of this great name, and often, in later times, it was used to quicken faith by the remembrance of the great deeds of God in the past. One instance may serve as a sample of the whole. "The Lord of Hosts is with us, the God of Jacob is our refuge." The first of these two names lays the foundation of our confidence in the thought of the boundless power of Him whom all the forces of the universe, personal and impersonal, angels and stars in their marshaled order, obey and serve. The second bids later generations claim as theirs all that the old history reveals as having belonged to the "world's gray fathers." They had no special prerogative of nearness or of possession. The arm that guided them is unwearied, and all the past is true still and will forevermore be true for all who love God. So the venerable name is full of promise and of hope for us: "the God of Jacob is our refuge."

2. The Shepherd

How that name sums up the lessons that Jacob had learned from the work of himself and of his sons! "Thy servants are shepherds," they said to Pharaoh; "both we, and also our sons." For fourteen long weary years he had toiled at that task. "In the day the drought consumed me, and the frost by night; and my sleep departed from mine eyes." And his own sleepless vigilance and patient endurance seem to him to be but shadows of the loving care, the watchful protection, the strong defense which "the God, who has been my Shepherd all my life long" had extended to him and his. Long before the shepherd king, who had been taken from the sheepcotes to rule over Israel, sang his immortal psalm, the same occupation had suggested the same thought to the shepherd patriarch. Happy they whose daily work may picture for them some aspect of God's care—or rather, happy they whose eyes are open to see the dim likeness of God's care which every man's earthly relations, and some part of his work, most certainly present.

There can be no need to draw out at length the thoughts which that sweet and familiar emblem has conveyed to so many generations. Loving care, wise guidance, fitting food are promised by it; and docile submission, close following at the Shepherd's heels, patience, innocence, meekness, trust are required. But I may emphasize for a moment the connection between the thought of "the mighty God of

Jacob" and that of "the Shepherd." The occupation, as we see it, does not call for a strong arm or much courage except now and then to wade through snow-drifts and dig out the buried and half-dead creature. But the shepherds whom Jacob knew had to be hardy, bold fighters. There were marauders lurking ready to sweep away a weakly guarded flock. There were wild beasts in the gorges of the hills. There was danger in the sun by day on these burning plains, and in the night the wolves prowled around the flock.

We remember how David's earliest exploits were against the lion and the bear, and how he felt that even his duel with the Philistine bully was not more formidable than these had been. If we will read into our English notions of a shepherd this element of danger and of daring, we shall feel that these two clauses are not to be taken as giving the contrasted ideas of strength and gentleness, but the connected ones of strength and therefore protection and security. We have the same connection in later echoes of this name. "Behold, the Lord God shall come with *strong* hand; He shall feed His flock like a shepherd."

And our Lord's use of the figure brings into all but exclusive prominence the good shepherd's conflict with the ravening wolves—a conflict in which he must not hesitate even "to lay down his life for the sheep." As long as the flock are here, amid dangers, and foes, and wild weather, the arm that guides must be an arm that guards; and none less mighty than the Mighty One of Jacob can be the Shepherd of men. But a higher fulfillment yet awaits this venerable emblem when in other pastures, where no lion nor any ravening beast shall come, the "Lamb, which is in the midst of the throne," and is Shepherd as well as Lamb, "shall feed them, and lead them by living fountains of waters."

3. The Stone of Israel

Here, again, we have a name that after-ages have caught up and cherished used for the first time. I suppose the Stone of Israel means much the same thing as the Rock. If so, that symbol, too, which is full of such large meanings was coined by Jacob. It is, perhaps, not fanciful to suppose that it owes its origin to the scenery of Palestine. The wild cliffs of the eastern region where Peniel lay or the savage fastnesses in the southern wilderness, a day's march from Hebron, where he lived so long came back to his memory amid the flat, clay land of Egypt; and their towering height, their immovable firmness, their cool shade, their safe shelter spoke to him of the unalterable might and impregnable defense which he had found in God. So there is in this name the same devout, reflective laying-hold upon experience which we have observed in the preceding.

There is also the same individualizing grasp of God as his very own for "Israel" here is, of course, to be taken not as the name of the nation but as his own name, and the intention of the phrase is evidently to express what God had been to him personally.

The general idea of this symbol is perhaps firmness, solidity. And that general idea may be followed out in various details. God is a rock for a foundation. Build your lives, your thoughts, your efforts, your hopes there. The house founded on the rock will stand though wind and rain from above smite it, and floods from beneath beat on it like battering-rams. God is a rock for a fortress. Flee to Him to hide, and your defense shall be the "munitions of rocks" which shall laugh to scorn all assault and never be stormed by any foe. God is a rock for shade and refreshment. Come close to Him from out of the scorching heat, and you will find coolness and verdure and moisture in the clefts when all outside that grateful shadow is parched and dry.

The word of the dying Jacob was caught up by the great lawgiver in his dying song. "Ascribe ye greatness to our God. He is the Rock." It reappears in the last words of the shepherd king whose grand prophetic picture of the true King is heralded by "The Rock of Israel spoke to me." It is heard once more from the lips of the greatest of the prophets in his glowing prophecy of the song of the final days: "Trust ye in the Lord forever; for in the Lord Jehovah is the Rock of Ages," as well as in his solemn prophecy of the Stone which God would lay in Zion. We hear it again from the lips that cannot lie. "Did ye never read in the Scriptures, The Stone which the builders rejected, the same is become the head-stone of the corner?" And for the last time the venerable metaphor which has cheered so many ages appears in the words of that Apostle who was "surnamed Cephas, which is by interpretation a stone." "To whom coming as unto a living stone, ye also as living stones are built up." As on some rocky site in Palestine where a thousand generations in succession have made their fortresses, one may see stones laid with the bevel that tells of early Jewish masonry, and above them Roman work, and higher still masonry of crusading times, and above it the building of today; so we, each age in our turn, build on this great rock foundation, dwell safe there for our little lives, and are laid to peaceful rest in a sepulcher in the rock. On Christ we may build. In Him we may dwell and rest secure. We may die in Jesus and be gathered to our own people who, having died, live in Him. And though so many generations have reared their dwellings on that great rock, there is ample room for us, too, to build. We have not to content ourselves with an uncertain foundation among the shifting rubbish of perished dwellings but can get down to the firm virgin rock for ourselves. None that have ever built there have been confounded. We clasp hands with all who have gone before us. At one end of the long chain this dim figure of the dying Jacob, amid the strange vanished life of Egypt, stretches out his withered hands to God the stone of Israel; at the other end, we lift up ours to Jesus, and cry:

> Rock of Ages! cleft for me,
> Let me hide myself in Thee.

The faith is one. One will be the answer and the reward. May it be yours and mine!

NOTES

The Lord God Omnipotent Reigneth

James S. Stewart (1896-1990) pastored three churches in Scotland before becoming professor of theology at the University of Edinburgh (1936) and then professor of New Testament (1946). But he is a professor who can preach, a scholar who can apply biblical truth to the needs of the common man, and a theologian who can make doctrine both practical and exciting. He has published several books of lectures and biblical studies including *A Man in Christ* and *Heralds of God*. His two finest books of sermons are *The Gates of New Life* and *The Strong Name*.

This sermon is taken from *The Gates of New Life*, published in Edinburgh in 1937 by T. & T. Clark.

James S. Stewart

6

THE LORD GOD OMNIPOTENT REIGNETH

Alleluia: for the Lord God omnipotent reigneth (Revelation 19:6).

WHAT IS THE biggest fact in life to you at this moment? What is the real center of your universe? "The biggest fact in life?" replies one man. "Well, I reckon it is my home. That, for me, is the center of everything." A very noble thing to be able to say! "The main fact in life to me," says a second, "is, without any shadow of doubt, my work. If you take that away from me, you take just everything." "The central thing for me," declares a third, "is health and happiness. As long as I have that, I am quite content. I can't bear to be unhappy." But what is your own answer?

I know what Jesus' answer was. Was it home? No—though none has ever hallowed home-life as Jesus hallowed it. Work, then? No—though none has toiled so terribly as the Son of God. Health and happiness? No—though none has been responsible for nearly so much clean happiness and mental and physical health as Jesus. The central fact in life to Jesus was none of these things. It was this—"The Lord God omnipotent reigneth!"

Is that your answer? More blessed than home, unspeakably blessed as home may be; more crucial than work, be that work never so urgent; more vital than health and happiness, though sometimes, especially when you lose them, happiness and health seem to be the only things that matter—greater and higher and deeper and more paramount than them all—the fact of God! The power behind every thought of your brain and every beat of your heart and every breath of your body—God! The element in which you live and move and have your being—God! The final, irreducible, and inescapable denominator of your

73

universe—God! That was the conviction on which Christ staked His life and marched to Calvary; that is the conviction which has inspired the breed of the saints; and that is the conviction which can turn very ordinary people like ourselves into men and women of whom Christ and the saints will not need to be ashamed; this conviction, strong as steel, firm as a rock, and stirring as a battle-cry: "The Lord God omnipotent reigneth!"

Now that cardinal conviction will be found, when you explore and examine it, to lead to three results. It involves three tremendous consequences, and as these concern us all most intimately, I would ask you to think of them now.

It means, first,

The Liberation of Life

It means a sense of absolute release. Release from what? Release from petty worries, to begin with. Everyone knows how sometimes things which are comparatively unimportant can obsess the mind and blot out all the sunshine. Here, let us say, is a man to whom some slight or some injustice has been administered, and he cannot get it out of his mind; he has not the grace to perform a surgical operation on that rankling thing, to cut it out and eradicate it; but he keeps on brooding and brooding about it with his mind continually coming back to it and going round it in wearisome circles—until the last vestige of peace of soul has been destroyed, his whole outlook on life warped, and all his sky obliterated by the mists and murky fogs of what is, from any spiritual standpoint, a wretched, insignificant triviality. Run and tell him, "The Lord God omnipotent reigneth!" Tell him to bring his worry into the light of that great truth, and just see how the fretting thing will fade and die. This, mark you, is not fancy nor hyperbole: it is proved experience, and the grace of the Lord Jesus Christ is in it.

The fact of the matter is, as Robert Browning said succinctly, "'Tis looking downward that makes one dizzy." The man who has his gaze riveted on the narrow little circle of his own experience, obsessed (like the poor creature in

Bunyan's dream) with the sticks and straws and dust of the floor, never thinking of the stars and the crown, cannot see life in true perspective. Oh, if only he would look away from all that—one long look into the face of the Lord God Almighty, if only he would take even five minutes in the morning to stabilize his soul by remembering Christ, how that would reinforce and liberate him! Yes, it is release— this great conviction—from the worries of life.

Notice, further, that it means release from the fears of life and especially from the fear of tasks that seem too great for us. Life is forever trying to make us lose our nerve and turn away from new responsibilities, saying like Jeremiah, "I can't do this! You must let me off: I am not the man for it. Please, God, get someone else!" Do you know what it means, when you have some particularly difficult duty confronting you, to lie awake through the night, revolving your anxious fears? You have that dreadful three-o'clock-in-the-morning feeling. "I'll never get through this! I'll never be able for it." But if religion cannot help us there, there is something wrong.

I remember Dr. John Mott telling some of us of a conversation which he had had with Dr. Cheng, the great Christian leader in China. "Would it not be a great thing," said Dr. Cheng, "for all of us Christians in China to unite, and go out and double the number of Protestant Church Christians within the next five years?" Dr. Mott asked, "How many are there now?" "Four hundred and thirty-five thousand," was the answer. "Well," said Dr. Mott, "it has taken over a hundred years to build in China a Christian Church of these dimensions, and do you now suggest the practicability of doubling that number in five years?" And Mott said that never would he forget the answer. "Why not?" exclaimed that gallant Chinese leader. "Why not?" And indeed, when a man has seen God—*why not*? "Impossible?" cried Richard Cobden when they had been criticizing as wild and fanciful and quite unfeasible his agitation for the repeal of the Corn Laws, "Impossible? If that is all that matters, I move we go ahead!" And again— why not, if "the Lord God omnipotent reigneth"? It is release from the fears of life.

Moreover, it is release from self-contempt. One fact which modern psychology has been driving home to our minds is this, that there are multitudes of people today who are losing half the happiness which God intended them to have and are being made quite unnecessarily miserable by inward repressions and conflicts and self-condemnations with which they do not know how to deal. And all the time there lies in religion (I am thinking, mark you, not of religion of the unbalanced, overemotional, unduly introspective type, for that may easily do more harm than good, but of the sane, healthy, objective religion of Jesus of Nazareth) the power to end the conflict and to set the prisoned soul free. What is the key with which Christ's religion unlocks the prison door? What but this, "The Lord God omnipotent reigneth"? "There," declares Jesus, "is the Father of whom you—even you—are a son. Son of man, stand upon your feet! Son of the omnipotent God, lift up your head and be free!"

Release from worry, release from fear, release from self-contempt—all that is bound up with this great central conviction of the faith. It means the liberation of life.

But that is not all. Notice now, in the second place, that it means

The Doom of Sin

It proclaims the ultimate defeat of evil in every shape and form.

Take this book of Revelation. You know the historic background of the book. It is a background of blood and smoke and martyrdom and reckless cynical laughter. Here you have the Rome of the Cæsars and the Church of the Galilean locked in the death-grapple. Here you have the mailed fist of Nero and Domitian smashing its way through the hopes and dreams of the saints. Here you have, in the words of an old psalmist, "the kings of the earth taking counsel together against the Lord, and against His Anointed, saying, 'Let us break their bands asunder, and cast away their cords from us!'" Here you have the second Babylon, mother of all the abominations of the earth, drunk with the blood of the friends of Jesus, laughing in

the intoxication of her triumph, shrieking with laughter
to see the poor, pathetic Body of Christ being crushed and
mangled and battered out of existence.

That is the background when this man takes up his
pen to write. And you and I look over his shoulder, wondering what his message is going to be. What can it be,
we think, but an elegy and a lament? "The battle is lost!
Our cause is ruined. There is nothing left but to sue for
mercy." Is that what we see him writing? No! But this—
flinging defiance at all the facts, and with the ring of iron
in it and the shout of the saints behind it—"Hallelujah!
Babylon is fallen, is fallen!" And why? What made the
man write like that? It was because at the back of the
visible world, at the back of Cæsar and all his pomp and
pride, he had seen something which Cæsar never saw,
something which spelt the doom of Cæsar and of all sin
like Cæsar's forever: a throne upraised above the earth,
and on the throne the Lord God omnipotent reigning!

We sometimes talk pessimistically about the future of
Christianity. We find ourselves wondering what will be
the ultimate issue in the warfare between good and evil.
Is it not possible that force and injustice may prevail, and
that the Jesus whom we love may go down at last before
powers that are too strong for Him? But to anyone who
has seen what this writer of Revelation saw, that is no
longer an open question. Evil is done for—already. "Well,"
someone may say incredulously, "it certainly does not look
like it. Look at the international scene. Look at our current literature. Look at the chaos in morals. See how evil
flaunts itself in the open, how it strikes its roots deeper
and still deeper." Yes, I know. But I know also this, that if
God is on the throne of the universe, then evil is doomed,
never has been anything else but doomed, doomed from
the foundations of the world!

Now no one was ever so sure of this as Jesus. There
was a day when the seventy followers whom He had sent
out into the surrounding villages to preach and to heal
returned to Him with their faces eager and glowing and
triumphant. "Master," they cried excitedly. "Master, it
works—this new power that has been given to us—it really

works! We have proved it. The darkest, foulest, most stubborn spirits are subject to us through Thy name!" Whereupon, says the evangelist, Jesus, hearing that glad news and realizing its deeper significance which even they could not quite fathom, had a sudden vision. "I beheld Satan," He exclaimed, "as lightning fall from heaven!" as though to say—"This message which you have brought settles and confirms and ratifies My hope. The power of darkness is broken, snapped, done for; and henceforth the initiative is with God!"

Or take the amazing scene which meets you at the end. Have you not gazed in wonder at the sight of Christ before His judges? How calm and self-possessed He was, far more self-possessed than Caiaphas, or Pilate, or Herod, or any of the other actors on that tragic stage! What was the secret of it? Was it just His innate heroism asserting itself? Was it just Christ's way of steeling His heart to be brave? Was it only a reckless contempt of death? No. It was the open vision that behind Caiaphas, and behind Pilate, and behind Herod, there was Someone else; and that it was not they nor any earthly governor who reigned in Jerusalem that night, but that Other, that watching, brooding Figure among the shadows—God! And Caiaphas, Pilate, Herod—who or what were they? Less than the dust beneath time's chariot-wheels. The Lord God omnipotent reigneth!

Such was the source of Jesus' heroism. And such, in the face of all the evils of the world, has been the source of the blessed optimism of the saints in every age. God is on the throne: therefore evil is doomed. "Here on this Rock," said Jesus once, "I will build my Church, and the gates of hell shall not prevail against it." Here on the Rock! That sudden cry of Christ, echoing down into the world of darkness, must have shaken that world to its foundations— like the thunderous chant of a great marching host, fair as the moon, clear as the sun, terrible as an army with banners. Francis Xavier, four hundred years ago, said a magnificent thing about the Christian mission to the Far East. "You may be very sure of one thing," he declared, "the devil will be tremendously sorry to see the Company of the Name of Jesus enter China." And then he went on—"Just imagine! A thing so vile as I am to bring down such a vast reputation as the devil's! What great glory to God!" Do you ask what is the mainspring of Christian hope and courage? It is the certainty that we are not fighting a losing battle; that evil, flaunt itself as it may, carries the seal of its own doom upon it; and that the real pull of the universe is on the side of the man who goes out for righteousness.

Fight on, then, you who have lost heart because your own conflict is so difficult, your tempter so strong and dogged and subtle. Fight on! It is your battle, not His. For the Lord God omnipotent reigneth.

We have seen, then, two decisive consequences bound up with our text: the liberation of life and the doom of sin. I ask you, finally, to observe that we have here

The Comfort of Sorrow

The man who wrote the twenty-ninth psalm, which we were reading today, had a marvelous sense of the dramatic. Do you remember how he sums up the great old story of the Flood of Genesis? He is looking back across the ages, and in imagination he can see that horror of the encroaching waters, rolling their waves higher and still higher, creeping up with slow, inexorable destruction and death, beating down all fragile human defenses built against them—until men and women, staring at those mounting waters, felt terror clutching at their throats for the end of the world seemed nigh. All that, the psalmist sees; but he sees something else as well. "The Lord," he cries, "sat as King at the Flood." Then, like a great shout—"Yea, the Lord sitteth King forever!"

And what of the floods of life? What shall we say of the days which every soul must know when, as Jesus put it, "the rain descends, and the floods come, and the winds blow and beat upon the house," until your whole structure of things, all your philosophy of life, is threatening to come toppling down? What about the happinesses you build for yourself—the plans you lay, the dreams you dream, the hopes you cherish, and the heart's desires you yearn for—and then, thundering and rolling mountain-high come the waves and the breakers, crashing down on that shore of dreams, leaving only some poor bits of wreckage behind? What then? Why then, blessed be God, the Lord sits as King at the flood, the Lord sitteth King forever! Which simply means that the heartbreaking things of life have meaning and purpose and grace in them for the Lord God omnipotent reigneth.

There was a terrible night out on the Galilean Lake when the sudden whirlwind blew, and the sea was lashed to fury, and the boat struggled in the troughs of the waves, and the disciples were telling themselves—"Our last hour has come: this is the end!" And there was Jesus, sleeping through it all. "Master, Master, careth Thou not that we perish!" But that night they learned by the grace of God this lesson—that there is something higher in human experience than life's waves and storms: there is a Christ who rules the waves! Have we discovered that? It is a great thing, when the floods begin and the desolation of sorrow comes beating down, to hear the divine *sursum corda*—up with your heart!—for the Lord sits King at the flood, your flood, and the Lord God omnipotent reigneth!

Did not Chesterton, in one of his most vivid poems, preach the same victory of the soul?

> Though giant rains put out the sun,
> Here stand I for a sign.
>
> Though Earth be filled with waters dark,
> My cup is filled with wine.
>
> Tell to the trembling priests that here
> Under the deluge rod,
>
> One nameless, tattered, broken man
> Stood up and drank to God.

There was once a flood called Calvary. And all the bitterness and ugliness, all the shame and sorrow of life entered into that flood and came beating around the brave soul of Jesus, sweeping Him down at last to the barbarity and infamy of the death of the cross. "What can God have been doing?" we want to ask. "Was He asleep? Or on a

journey? Or was He dead?" No! The Lord was sitting as
King at the flood, that surging flood of Calvary; and out of
that grim cross He has brought the salvation of the world.
Tell me—if God did that with the cross of Jesus, do you
think your cross can be too difficult for Him to deal with
and to transfigure? He can make it shine with glory.

Do you believe it? My friend, here is surely the final
victory of faith—to be able to say, "The Lord God omnipotent reigneth," to cry it aloud, not only when life is kind
and tender and smiling, and the time of the singing of
birds is come and the flowers appear on the earth, but
even more when the night is dark, and you are far from
home, and the proud waters are going over your soul; to
cry it then, not weakly nor diffidently nor uncertainly, but
vehemently and passionately and with the ring of faith in
every syllable of it—"The Lord God omnipotent reigneth.
Hallelujah!"

This is the Lord God who has come again to the gate of
your life and mine today. This is the Lord God who claims
the right to reign, and from whose patient, haunting pursuit we can never in this world get free. Behold, He stands
at the door and knocks. While the sands of time are running out and the hurrying days mold our destiny, He
stands at the door and knocks. Tenderer than the kiss of
a little child, mightier than the flashing lightnings of heav-
en, He stands at the door and knocks. What will our
answer be? "You, out there at the door, you who have
been haunting and troubling me all these years—begone,
and leave me in peace!" Is that it? Or is it not rather this?
"Blessed and glorious Lord Almighty, dear loving Christ
of God—come! Come now. My life is yours. See, here is
the throne. Oh, Christ, take your power—and reign!"

Jehovah Rophi

Charles Haddon Spurgeon (1834-1892) is undoubtedly the most famous minister of modern times. Converted in 1850, he united with the Baptists and soon began to preach in various places. He became pastor of the Baptist church in Waterbeach in 1851, and three years later he was called to the decaying Park Street Church, London. Within a short time, the work began to prosper, a new church was built and dedicated in 1861, and Spurgeon became London's most popular preacher. In 1855, he began to publish his sermons weekly; and today they make up the fifty-seven volumes of *The Metropolitan Tabernacle Pulpit*. He founded a pastor's college and several orphanages.

This sermon is taken from *The Metropolitan Tabernacle Pulpit*, Volume 28.

Charles Haddon Spurgeon

7

JEHOVAH ROPHI

I am the Lord that healeth thee (Exodus 15:26).

WE SHALL CONSIDER this passage in its connection for I
have no doubt that the miracle at Marah was intended to
be a very instructive illustration of the glorious title which
is here claimed by the covenant God of Israel: "I am Jehovah-Rophi, the Lord that healeth thee." The illustration
introduces the sermon of which this verse is the text. The
healing of the bitter waters is the parable of which the
line before us is the lesson.

How different is the Lord to His foes and to His friends.
His presence is light to Israel and darkness to Egypt.
Egypt only knew Jehovah as the Lord that plagues and
destroys those who refuse to obey Him. Is not this the
Lord's memorial in Egypt that He cut Rahab and wounded the dragon? He overthrew their armies at the Red Sea
and drowned their hosts beneath the waves; but to His
own people, in themselves but very little superior to the
Egyptians, God is not the terrible avenger consuming His
adversaries, but "Jehovah that healeth thee." Their mental and moral diseases were almost as great as those of
the Egyptians whom the Lord cut off from before Him,
but He spared His chosen for His covenant sake. He bared
the sword of justice against rebellious Pharaoh, and then
He turned His tender, healing hand upon His own people
to exercise toward them the heavenly surgery of His grace.
Israel knew Him as the Lord Who heals, and Egypt knew
Him as the Lord Who smites. Let us adore the grace
which makes so wide a difference, the sovereign grace
which brings salvation unto Israel, and let us confess our
own personal obligations to the mercy which has not dealt
with *us* after our sins, nor rewarded *us* according to our
iniquities.

Again, how differently does God deal with His own people from what we should have expected. He is a God of surprises, He does things which we do not expect. God deals with us not according to our conception of His ways, but according to His own wisdom and prudence; for as the heavens are high above the earth, so high are His thoughts above our thoughts. You would not have supposed that a people for whom God had given Egypt as a ransom would have been led into the wilderness of Shur; neither would you have guessed that a people so near to Him that He cleft the sea and made them walk between two glassy walls dry shod, would have been left for three days without water. You naturally expect to see the chosen tribes brought right speedily into a condition of comfort; or, if there must be a journey before they reach the land that flows with milk and honey, you look at once for the smitten rock and the flowing stream, the manna and the quails, and all things else which they can desire. How singular it seems that after having done such a great marvel for them, the Lord should cause them to thirst beneath a burning sky, and that, too, when they were quite unprepared for it, being quite new to desert privations, having lived so long by the river of Egypt where they drank of sweet water without stint. We read at other times, "Thou, Lord, didst send a plenteous rain, whereby thou didst refresh thine inheritance when it was weary"; but here we meet with no showers, no brooks gushed forth below, and no rain dropped from above. Three days without water is a severe trial when the burning sand is below and the blazing sky is above. Yet the Lord's people in some way or other are sure to be tried; theirs is no holiday parade, but a stern march by a way which flesh and blood would never have chosen.

The Egyptians found enough water, and even too much of it, for they were drowned in the sea, but the well-beloved Israelites had no water at all. So is it with the wicked man; he often has enough of wealth, and too much of it, till he is drowned in sensual delights and perishes in floods of prosperity. He has his portion in this life, and in that portion he is lost like Pharaoh in the proud waters.

Often the Lord's people are made to know the pinch of poverty, their lives are made wretched by sore bondage, and they faint for a morsel of bread. They drink from a bitter fountain which fills their inward parts with gall and wormwood. They are afflicted very much, almost to the breaking of their hearts. One of them said, "All the day long have I been plagued, and chastened every morning." They lie at the rich man's gate full of sores while the ungodly man is clothed in scarlet and fares sumptuously every day. This is God's strange way of dealing with His own people. He Himself hath said, "As many as I love I rebuke and chasten." "He scourgeth every son whom he receiveth." Thus He made His people know that the wilderness was not their rest nor their home for they could not even find such a common necessity as water wherewith to quench their thirst.

He made them understand that the promised brooks that flowed with milk and honey were not in the wilderness but must be found on the other side of Jordan in the land which God had given to their fathers, and they must journey thither with weary feet. "This is not your rest" was the lesson of their parched lips in the three days' march. You know what teaching there is in all this for your experience answers to it. Do not marvel, beloved, if with all your joy over your vanquished sin, which shall be seen by you no more forever, you yet have to lament your present grievous want. The children of Israel cried, "What shall we drink?" This was a wretched sequel to "Sing unto the Lord, for He hath triumphed gloriously." Have you never made the same descent?

If you are in poverty you are, no doubt, tempted to put that trinity of questions, "What shall we eat? What shall we drink? And wherewithal shall we be clothed?" You are not the first to whom this temptation has happened. Do not marvel at all if up from the triumph of the Red Sea, with a song in your mouth and a timbrel in your hand, you ascend into the great and terrible wilderness, and enter upon the land of drought. This way lies Canaan, and this way you must go. Through much tribulation we must enter the kingdom, and therefore let us set our minds to it.

By this grievous test the Lord was proving His people and causing them to see what was in their hearts. They would have known no wilderness without if there had not been a wilderness within, neither had there been a drought of water for their mouths if the Lord had not seen a drought of grace in their souls. We are fine birds till our feathers are ruffled, and then what a poor figure we cut! We are just a mass of diseases and a bundle of disorders, and unless grace prevents we are the sure prey of death. O Lord, we pray to be proved, but we little know what it means!

Let this suffice for an introduction, and then let our text come in with comfort to our hearts, "I am the Lord that healeth thee." It was to illustrate this great name of God that the tribes were brought into so painful a condition; and indeed all the experience of a believer is meant to glorify God, that the believer himself may see more of God, and that the world outside may also behold the glory of the Lord. Therefore the Lord leadeth His people up and down in the wilderness, and therefore He makes them cry out because there is no water—all to make them behold His power, and His goodness, and His wisdom. Our lives are the canvas upon which the Lord paints His own character.

We shall try this morning to set forth before you, by the help of the divine Spirit, this grand character of God, that He is the God that healeth us. First, we shall notice *the healing of our circumstances*, dwelling upon that in order the better to set forth the greater fact, "I am the Lord that healeth *thee*." Secondly, we shall remember *the healing of our bodies* which is here promised to obedient Israel, and we shall set forth that truth in order to bring out our third point which is *the healing of our souls*: "I am the Lord that healeth *thee*"—not thy circumstances only, nor thy bodily diseases only, but thyself, thy soul, thy truest self for there is the worst bitterness, there is the sorest disease, and there shall the grandest power of God be shown to thee and to all who know thee.

I. The Glorious Jehovah Shows His Healing Power upon Our Circumstances

The fainting Israelites thought that when they came to

Marah they should slake their thirst. Often enough the mirage had mocked them as it does all thirsty travelers; they thought that they saw before them flowing rivers and palm trees, but as they rushed forward they found nothing but sand for the mirage was deluding them. At last, however, the waters of Marah were fairly within sight, and they were not a delusion; here was real water, and they were sure of it. No doubt they rushed forward helter-skelter, each man eager to drink, and what must have been their disappointment when they found that they could not endure it.

A thirsty man will drink almost anything, but this water was so bitter that it was impossible for them to receive it. I do not read that they had murmured all the three days of their thirsty march, but this disappointment was too much for them. The relief which seemed so near was snatched away, the cup was dashed from their lips, and they began to murmur against Moses and so in truth against God. Here was the proof of their imperfection: they were impatient and unbelieving.

Have we not too often fallen into the same sin? Brethren, let your conscience answer! When you have felt a sharp affliction, and it has continued long, and you have been wearied out with it, you have at length seen a prospect of escape but that prospect has completely failed you. What woe is this! When the friend you so surely relied upon tells you that he can do nothing, when the physician upon whom you put such reliance informs you that his medicine has not touched the malady, when the last expedient that you could adopt to save yourself from bankruptcy, the last arrow in your quiver has missed the mark—how your spirit has sunk within you in dire despair! Then your heart has begun to wound itself, like the scorpion, with its own sting. You have felt as if you were utterly spent and ready for the grave. The last trial was too much for you, and you could bear up no longer.

Happy have you been if under such conditions you have not been left to give way to murmuring against God. These poor Israelites were in a very pitiable condition. There was the water before them, but its horrible flavor made them shrink from a second taste. Have you not experienced the same? You have obtained that which you thought would deliver you, but it has not availed you. You looked for light and beheld darkness; for refreshment and beheld an aggravated grief. The springs of earth are brackish until Jehovah heals them; they increase the thirst of the man who too eagerly drinks of them. "Cursed is he that trusteth in man, and maketh flesh his arm."

Now, dear friends, in answer to prayer God has often healed your bitter waters and made them sweet. I am about to appeal to your personal experience, you who are truly pilgrims under the guidance of your heavenly Lord. Has it not been so with you? I should have no difficulty in refreshing your memories about Marah for very likely its bitterness is in your mouth even now, and you cannot forget your sorrow. But just now I wish to refresh your memories about what came of that sorrow. Did not God deliver you? Did He not, when you cried to Him, come to your rescue? I appeal to facts, which may be stubborn things, but they are also rich encouragements.

Has not the Lord oftentimes made our bitter waters sweet *by changing our circumstances altogether*? When the poor in heart have been oppressed, God has taken away the oppressor or else taken the heart away from the oppression. When you have been in great straits and could not see which way to steer, has not the Lord Jesus seemed to open before you a wider channel, or Himself to steer your vessel through all the intricacies of the narrow river and bring you where you would come? Have you not noticed in your lives that most remarkable changes have taken place at times when anguish took hold upon you? I can bear my witness, if you cannot, that the Lord has great healing power in the matter of our trials and griefs. He has changed my circumstances in providence and in many ways altered the whole aspect of affairs.

On other occasions the Lord has not removed the circumstances, and yet He has turned sorrow into joy for He has *put into them a new ingredient* which has acted as an antidote to the acrid flavor of your affliction. You were not allowed to leave the shop, but there came a fresh manager who shielded you from persecution; you were not permitted to quit your business, but there came a wonderful improvement in your trade, and this reconciled you to the long hours. You were not made to be perfectly healthy, but you were helped to a medicine which much assuaged the sharpness of the pain; thus has your Marah been sweetened. Have you not found it so? The weight of your affliction was exceeding great, but the Lord found a counterpoise, and by placing a weight of holy joy in the other scale, He lifted up your load, and its weight was virtually taken away. You have been at Marah, but even there you have been able to drink for a something has been put into the waters of afflictive providence which has made them endurable.

And where this has not been done the Lord has by a heavenly art made your bitter waters sweet *by giving you more satisfaction with the divine will*, more submission, more acquiescence in what the Lord has ordained. After all, this is the most effectual remedy. If I cannot bring my circumstances to my mind, yet if God helps me to bring my mind to my circumstances, the matter is made right. There is a degree of sweetness about pain, and poverty, and shame when once you feel, "The loving Lord ordained all this for me: my tribulation is of His appointing." Then the soul, feeling that the affliction comes from a Father's hand, accepts it, and kicks against the pricks no longer. Surely, then, the bitterness of life or of death will be past when the mind is subdued to the Eternal will. These people said, "What shall we drink?" and they would have concluded that Moses was mocking them if he had answered, "You shall drink the bitter water." They would have said, "We cannot bear it; we remember the sweet water of the Nile; and we cannot endure this nauseous stuff." But Moses would have said, "Yes, you will drink that, and nothing else but that, and it will become to you all that you want." Even so, beloved, you may have quarreled with your circumstances, and said, "I must have a change; I cannot longer bear this trial." Has not the Lord of His grace changed your mind and so influenced your will that you have really found comfort in that which was uncomfortable and contentment in that which made you discontented? Have you never said when under tribulation, "I could not have believed it; I am perfectly happy under my trial, and yet when I looked forward to it, I dreaded it beyond measure. I said it would be the death of me, but now I find that by these things men live and in all this is the life of my spirit." We exclaim with Jacob, "All these things are against me," but the Lord gives us more grace, and we see that all things work together for good, and we bless the Lord for His afflicting hand. So you see the Lord Jehovah heals our bitter waters and makes our circumstances endurable to our sanctified minds.

Brethren, all this which you have experienced should be to you a proof of God's power to make everything that is bitter sweet. The depravity of your nature will yield to the operations of His grace, the corruptions that are within you will yet be subdued, and you shall enter into the fullest communion with God in Christ Jesus. I know you shall because the Lord is unchangeable in power, and what He has done in one direction, He can and will do in another. Your circumstances were so terrible, and yet God helped you; and now your sins, your inbred sins which are so dreadful, He will help you against them and give you power over them. You shall overcome the power of evil; by His grace you shall be sanctified, and you shall manifest the sweetness of holiness instead of the bitterness of self. Cannot you believe it? Does not God's power exhibited in providence around you prove that He has power enough to do great things within you by His grace?

Moreover, should not this healing of your circumstances be to you a pledge that God will heal you as to your inner spirit? He who brought you through the sea and drowned your enemies will also drown your sins 'till you shall sing, "The depths have covered them: there is not one of them left." He who turned your Marah into sweetness will yet turn all your sense of sin into a sense of pardon; all the bitterness of your regret and the sharpness of your repentance shall yet be turned into the joy of faith, and you shall be full of delight in the perfect reconciliation which comes by the precious blood of Christ.

Sustaining providences are to the saints sure pledges of grace. The sweetened water is a picture of a sweetened nature; I had almost said it is a type of it. God binds Himself by the gracious deliverances of His providence to give you equal deliverances of grace. It is joyous to say, "He is the Lord that healed my circumstances," but how much better to sing of His name as "The Lord that healeth *thee.*" Do not be contented till you reach to that; but do be confident that He who healed Marah will heal you; He who has helped you to rejoice in Him in all your times of trouble will sustain you in all your struggles with sin till you shall more sweetly and more loudly praise His blessed name.

Let us now proceed a step further. As we have spoken of God's healing our circumstances, so now we have to think of

II. The Lord's Healing Our Bodies

Why are diseases and pains left in the bodies of God's people? Our bodies are redeemed for Christ has redeemed our entire manhood, but if Christ be in us the body is still dead because of sin even though the spirit is alive because of righteousness. It is not till the resurrection that we shall enjoy the full result of the redemption of the body. Resurrection will accomplish for our bodies what regeneration has done for our souls. We were born again. Yes, but that divine work was exercised only upon our spiritual nature; our bodies were not born again; hence they still abide under the liability of disease, decay, and death though even these evils have been turned into blessings. This frail, sensitive, and earthly frame, which Paul calls "this vile body," grows weary and worn, and by-and-by it will fade away and die unless the Lord shall come; and even if He should come, this feeble fabric must be totally changed for flesh and blood as they now are cannot inherit the kingdom of God, neither can corruption dwell with incorruption. Even unto this day the body is under death because of sin and is left so on purpose to remind us of the effects of sin that we may feel within ourselves what sin has done and may the better guess at what sin would have done if we had remained under it for the pains of hell would have been ours forever. These griefs of body are meant, I say, to make us recollect what we owe to the redemption of our Lord Jesus and so to keep us humble and grateful. Aches and pains are also sent to keep us on the wing for heaven even as thorns in the nest drive the bird from its sloth. They make us long for the land where the inhabitant shall no more say, I am sick.

Yet the Lord does heal our bodies. First He heals them *by preventing sickness*. A prevention is better than cure. The text says, "If thou wilt diligently hearken to the voice of the Lord thy God, and wilt do that which is right in His sight, and wilt give ear to His commandments, and keep all His statutes, I will put none of these diseases upon thee, which I have brought upon the Egyptians: for I am the Lord that healeth thee." It is concerning this self-same healing Lord that we read, "Thou shalt not be afraid for the terror by night; nor for the darkness; nor for the destruction that wasteth at noonday. A thousand shall fall at thy side and ten thousand at thy right hand; but it shall not come nigh thee. Only with thine eyes shalt thou behold and see the reward of the wicked. Because thou hast made the Lord, which is my refuge, even the most High, thy habitation; there shall no evil befall thee, neither shall any plague come nigh thy dwelling."

Do we sufficiently praise God for guarding us from disease? I am afraid that His preserving care is often forgotten. Men will go thirty or forty years almost without an illness and forget the Lord in consequence. That which should secure gratitude creates indifference. When we have been ill we come up to the house of the Lord and desire to return thanks because of our recovery; ought we not to give thanks when we are not ill and do not need to be recovered? Should it not be to you healthy folk a daily cause of gratitude to God that He keeps away those pains which would keep you awake all night and wards off those sicknesses which would cause your beauty to consume away like the moth?

But we see this healing hand of the Lord more conspicuously when, like Hezekiah, we have been sick and have been restored. Sometimes we lie helpless and hopeless like dust ready to return to its fellow dust; we are incapable of exertion and ready to be dissolved. Then if the Lord renews our youth and takes away our sickness, we do praise His name; and so we ought for it is not the doctor, it is not the medicine—these are but the outward means; it is the Lord who is the true Physician, and unto Jehovah-Rophi be the praise. "I am the Lord that healeth thee." Let those of us who have been laid aside and have been again allowed to walk abroad, lift up our hearts and our voices in thanksgiving to the Lord who forgives all our iniquities, who heals all our diseases.

According to the analogy of the healing of Marah, the Lord does this by means for He cast a tree into the water. Those who will use no medicine whatever certainly have no Scriptural warrant for their conduct. Even where cures are given to faith, yet the Apostle says, "Is any sick? Let him send for the elders of the church, and let them pray over him, anointing him with oil in the name of the Lord." The anointing with oil was the proper medicine of the day and possibly a great deal better medicine than some of the drugs which are used nowadays. To the use of this anointing the promise is given, "and the prayer of faith shall raise the sick." Hezekiah was miraculously healed, but the Lord said, "take a lump of figs, and lay it upon the sore." God could have spoken a word and turned Marah sweet, but He did not choose to do so; He would exercise the faith and obedience of His people by bidding them cast a tree into the waters. The use of means is not to hinder faith but to try it. Still, it is the Lord who works the cure, and this is the point which is so often forgotten. Oh, come let us sing unto Jehovah Who hath said, "I am the Lord that healeth thee." Do not attribute to secondary means that which ought to be ascribed to God alone. His fresh air, and warm sun, or bracing wind, and refreshing showers do more for our healing than we dream of, or if medicine be used, it is He who gives virtue to the drugs and so by His own Almighty hand works out our cure. As one who has felt His restoring hand, I will personally sing unto Him who is the health of my countenance and my God.

Note this, that in every healing of which we are the subjects, we have a pledge of the resurrection. Every time a man who is near the gates of death rises up again, he enjoys a kind of rehearsal of that grand rising when from beds of dust and silent clay the perfect saints shall rise at the trump of the archangel and the voice of God. We ought to gather from our restorations from serious and perilous sickness a proof that the God who brings us back from the gates of the grave can also bring us back from the grave itself whenever it shall be His time to do so.

This should also be a yet further proof to us that if He can heal our bodies, the Lord can heal our souls. If this poor worm's meat which so readily decays can be revived, so can the soul which is united to Christ and quickened with His life; and if the Almighty Lord can cast out evils from this poor dust and ashes which must ultimately be dissolved, much more can He cast out all manner of evils from that immaterial spirit which is yet to shine in the brightness of the glory of God. Wherefore both from His healing your woes and from His healing your bodies, gather power to believe in the fact that He will heal your mental, moral, and spiritual diseases, and already lift up your hearts with joy as you sing of Jehovah Rophi, "The Lord that healeth *thee*."

> Sinners of old thou didst receive,
>   With comfortable words and kind,
> Their sorrows cheer, their wants relieve,
>   Heal the diseased, and cure the blind,
>
> And art thou not the Savior still,
>   In every place and age the same?
> Hast thou forgot thy gracious skill,
>   Or lost the virtue of thy name?
>
> Faith in thy changeless name I have;
>   The good, the kind Physician, thou
> Art able now our souls to save,
>   Art willing to restore them now.
>
> Though eighteen hundred years are past
>   Since thou didst in the flesh appear,
> Thy tender mercies ever last;
>   And still thy healing power is here!

> Wouldst thou the body's health restore,
> And not regard the sin-sick soul?
> The sin-sick soul thou lov'st much more,
> And surely thou shalt make it whole.

The healing of Marah and the healing of the body are placed before the text, and they shed a light upon it. They place this name of the Lord in a golden frame and cause us to look upon it with the greater interest.

Now we come to

III. The Healing of Our Souls

The Lord our God will heal our spirits, and He will do it in somewhat the same manner as that in which He healed Marah. How was that? First, He made the people know how bitter Marah was. There was no healing for that water till they had tasted it and discovered that it was too brackish to be endured; but after they knew its bitterness then the Lord made it sweet to them. So is it with your sin, my brother. It must become more and more bitter to you. You will have to cry out, "O wretched man that I am, who shall deliver me?" You yourself. The creature must be made distasteful to you and all trusts that come of it for God's way is first to kill and then to make alive, first to wound and then to heal. He begins by making Marah to be Marah, and afterward He makes it sweet.

What next? The next thing was: there was prayer offered. I do not know whether any of the people possessed faith in God, but if so, they had a prayerless faith, and God does not work in answer to prayerless faith. "Oh," says one, "I am perfectly sanctified." How do you know? "Because I believe I am." That will never do. Is a man rich because he believes he is? Will sickness vanish if I believe myself to be well? Some even think it useless to pray because they feel sure of having the blessing. That putting aside of prayer is a dangerous piece of business altogether. If there is not the cry to God for the blessing, yes, and the daily cry for keeping and for sanctification, the mercy will not come. Again, I say, healing comes not to a prayerless faith. You may believe what you like, but God will only hear you when you pray. Faith must pour itself out in prayer before the blessing will be poured into the soul. Moses cried, and he obtained the blessing/the people did not cry, and they would have been in an evil case had it not been for Moses. We must come to crying and praying before we shall receive sanctification which is the making whole of our spirits.

Marah became sweet through the introduction of something outside of itself—a tree, I know not of what kind. The rabbis say that it was a bitter tree and naturally tended to make the water more bitter still. However that may be, I cannot imagine any tree in all the world, bitter or sweet, which could have power to sweeten such a quantity of water as must have been at Marah. The transaction was miraculous, and the tree was used merely as the instrument and no further. But I do know a tree which, if put into the soul, will sweeten all its thoughts and desires; and Jesus knew that tree, that tree whereon He died and shed His blood as a victim for our sin.

If the merit of the cross be imputed to us, and the spirit of the cross be introduced into our nature; if we trust the Lord Jesus, and rest upon Him; yes, if we become cross-bearers, and our soul is crucified to the world, then we shall find a marvelous change of our entire nature. Whereas we were full of vice, the Crucified One will make us full of virtue; and whereas we were bitter toward God, we shall be sweet to Him, and even Christ will be refreshed as He drinks of our love, as He drinks of our trust, as He drinks of our joy in Him. Where all was acrid, sharp, and poisonous, everything shall become pure, delicious, and refreshing. We must first experience a sense of bitterness, then cry out to the Lord in prayer, and then yield an obedient faith which puts the unlikely tree into the stream, and then the divine power shall be put forth upon us by Him who saith, "I am the Lord that healeth thee."

The inner healing is set forth as in a picture in the sweetening of the bitter pools of Marah. I know I am right in saying so because we are told of Moses, "There he made for them a statute and an ordinance, and there he proved them."

Again the task of turning Marah sweet was a very difficult one. No human power could have achieved it; and even so the task of changing our nature is not only difficult but impossible to us. We must be born again, not of the will of man nor of blood, nor of the will of the flesh, but of God. There was no turning Marah sweet by any means within the reach of Moses or the myriads that came up with him out of Egypt. This wonder must come from Jehovah's hand. So is the change of our nature a thing beyond all human might. Who can make his own heart clean? God must work this marvel. We must be born again from above, or else we shall remain in the gall of bitterness even unto the end.

But yet the work was very easy to God. How simple a thing it was just to take a tree and cast it into the bitter water and find it sweet at once. Even so it is an easy thing to God to make us a new heart and a right spirit and so to incline us to everything that is right and good. What a blessing is this! If I had to make myself holy, I must despair; and if I had to make myself perfect and keep myself so, it would never be done; but the Lord Jehovah can do it and has already begun to do it. Things which I once hated I now love; all things have become new. Simple faith in Jesus Christ, the putting of the cross into the stream, does it all and does it at once, too, and does it so effectually that there is no return of the bitterness, but the heart remains sweet and pure before the living God.

The task was completely accomplished. The people came and drank of Marah just as freely as they afterward drank of Elim or of the water that leaped from the smitten rock. So God can and will complete in us the change of our nature. Paul says, "I am persuaded that he that hath begun a good work in you will perfect it until the day of Christ." The Lord has not begun to sweeten us a little with the intent of leaving us in a half-healed condition, but He will continue the process till we are without trace of defilement, made pure and right in His sight.

This work is one which greatly glorifies God. If the change of Marah's water made the people praise God, much more will the change of nature make us adore Him forever and ever. We are going to be exalted, brethren, by-and-by, to the highest place in the universe next to God. Man, poor, sinful man, is to be so changed as to be able to stand side by side with Christ, Who has for that very purpose taken upon Himself human nature. We are to be above the angels. The highest seraphim shall be less privileged than the heirs of salvation. Now, the tendency to pride would be very strong upon us only that we shall always recollect what we used to be and what power it was that has made us what we are. This will make it safe for God to glorify His people.

There will be no fear of our sullying God's honor or setting ourselves up in opposition to Him as did Lucifer of old. It shall never be said of any spirit washed in the precious blood of Jesus, "How art thou fallen from heaven, O son of the morning!" for the process through which we shall pass in turning our bitterness to sweetness will fill us with perpetual adoration and with constant reverence of the unspeakably mighty grace of God.

Will it not be so, brethren? Do not your impulses even now lead you to feel that when you gain your promised crowns, the first thing you will joyfully do will be to cast them at the feet of Jesus and say, "Not unto us, not unto us, but unto thy name be glory forever and ever"? That sweetened Marah was all of God; our renewed nature shall be all of God. We shall not be able to take the slightest particle of credit to ourselves, nor shall we wish to do so.

Brethren, the Lord will do it; He will be sure to do it because it will glorify His name. Let us draw comfort from this fact: there will be no interfering with the Lord by a rival claimant to honor, no idolatry in us taking away part of His praises; therefore He will do it and change our bitterness into perfect sweetness. Blessed be His name, He can do it; nothing will baffle the skill of "the Lord that healeth thee." Whenever I am cast down under a sense of corruption, I always like to get a hold of this divine name, "The Lord that healeth thee." "Thanks be to God who giveth us the victory through our Lord Jesus

Christ." "Faithful is he that hath called you, who also will
do it," says the apostle. He has not undertaken what He
will fail to perform. Jehovah Who made heaven and earth
has undertaken to make us perfect and effectually to heal
us; therefore let us be confident that it will assuredly be
accomplished, and we shall be presented without spot
before God.

He who heals us is a God so glorious that He will
certainly perform the work. There is none like unto the
Omnipotent One! He is able to subdue all things unto
Himself. His wisdom, power, and grace can so work upon
us that where sin abounded, grace shall much more
abound.

> Thou canst o'ercome this heart of mine;
>   Thou wilt victorious prove;
> For everlasting strength is thine,
>   And everlasting love.
>
> Thy powerful Spirit shall subdue
>   Unconquerable sin;
> Cleanse this foul heart, and make it new,
>   And write thy law within.

He is a God Who loves us so and makes us so precious in
His sight that He gave Egypt for our ransom, Ethiopia
and Seba for us. A God so loving will surely perfect that
which concerns us. Moreover, a God so fond of purity, a
God Who hates sin so intensely and Who loves righteousness so fervently will surely cleanse the blood of His own
children. He must and will make His own family pure.
"This people have I formed for myself: they shall show
forth my praise." The devil cannot hinder that decree.
"They shall," says God, and they shall, too, whatever shall
stand in their way. They must and they shall show forth
God's praise.

Now, as you have believed in God for your justification
and found it in Christ, so believe in God for your sanctification that He will work in you to will and to do according
to His good pleasure; that He will exterminate in you the
very roots of sin; that He will make you like Himself,
without taint or speck; and that, as surely as you are

trusting in Christ, you shall be whiter than snow, pure as the infinite Jehovah, and you shall stand with His First-born, accepted in the Beloved. My soul seems to grasp this and to hold it all the more firmly because the Lord has turned my bitter circumstances into sweetness, and He has healed the sickness of my body. Because of these former mercies I know that He will heal the sickness of my spirit, and I shall be whole, that is to say holy, without spot or trace of sin, and so shall I be forever with the Lord. "Wherefore comfort one another with these words."

Brethren, if the Lord has taken you into His hospital and healed you, do not forget other sick folk. Freely ye have received, freely give. Give today to the hospitals in which so many of the poor are cared for and succored. Do it for Jesus sake, and may the Lord accept your offerings.

NOTES

Jehovah Jireh

Alexander MacLaren (1826-1910) was one of Great Britain's most famous preachers. While pastoring the Union Chapel, Manchester (1858-1903), he became known as "the prince of expository preachers." Rarely active in denominational or civic affairs, MacLaren invested his time in studying the Word in the original and sharing its truths with others in sermons that are still models of effective expository preaching. He published a number of books of sermons and climaxed his ministry by publishing his monumental *Expositions of Holy Scripture*.

This message is taken from MacLaren's *Expositions of Holy Scripture*, Volume 1 (Baker Book House, 1974).

Alexander MacLaren

8

JEHOVAH JIREH

And Abraham called the name of that place Jehovah Jireh (that is, The Lord will provide) (Genesis 22:14).

As THESE TWO, Abraham and Isaac, were traveling up the hill, the son bearing the wood and the father with the sad burden of the fire and the knife, the boy said: "Where is the lamb?" and Abraham, thrusting down his emotion and steadying his voice, said: "My son, God will provide Himself a lamb." When the wonderful issue of the trial was plain before him and he looked back upon it, the one thought that rose to his mind was of how, beyond his meaning, his words had been true. So he named that place by a name that spoke nothing of his trial but everything of God's provision—"The Lord will see," or "The Lord will provide."

What the Words Mean

The words have become proverbial and threadbare as a commonplace of Christian feeling. But it may be worth our while to ask for a moment what it was exactly that Abraham expected the Lord to provide. We generally use the expression in reference to outward things and see in it the assurance that we shall not be left without the supply of the necessities for which, because God has made us to feel them, He has bound Himself to make provision. And most blessedly true is that application of them, and many a Christian heart in days of famine has been satisfied with the promise when the bread that was given has been scant.

But there is a meaning deeper than that in the words. It is true, thank God! that we may cast all our anxiety about all outward things upon Him in the assurance that He who feeds the ravens will feed us, and that if lilies can blossom

103

into beauty without care, we shall be held by our Father of more value than these. But there is a deeper meaning in the provision spoken of here. What was it that God provided for Abraham? What is it that God provides for us? A way to discharge the arduous duties which, when they are commanded, seem all but impossible for us and which, the nearer we come to them, look the more dreadful and seem the more impossible. And yet, when the heart has yielded itself in obedience and we are ready to do the thing that is enjoined, there opens up before us a possibility provided by God, and strength comes to us equal to our day, and some unexpected gift is put into our hand which enables us to do the thing of which Nature said: "My heart will break before I can do it"; and in regard to which even Grace doubted whether it was possible for us to carry it through. If our hearts are set in obedience to the command, the farther we go on the path of obedience, the easier the command will appear, and to try to do it is to ensure that God will help us to do it.

This is the main provision that God makes, and it is the highest provision that He can make for there is nothing in this life that we need so much as to do the will of our Father in heaven. All outward wants are poor compared with that. The one thing worth living for, the one thing which in being secured we are blessed and being missed we are miserable, is compliance in heart with the commandment of our Father, and the compliance wrought out in life. So, of all gifts that He bestows upon us and of all the abundant provision out of His rich storehouses is not this the best, that we are made ready for any required service? When we get to the place we shall find some lamb "caught in the thicket by its horns"; and heaven itself will supply what is needful for our burnt offering.

And then there is another thought here which, though we cannot certainly say it was in the speaker's mind, is distinctly in the historian's intention, "The Lord will provide." Provide what? The lamb for the burnt offering which He has commanded. It seems probable that that bare mountaintop which Abraham saw from afar and named Jehovah Jireh, was the mountain-top on which afterward the Temple was built. And perhaps the wood was piled for the altar on that very piece of primitive rock which still stands visible, though Temple and altar have long since gone, and which for many a day was the place of the altar on which the sacrifices of Israel were offered. It is no mere forcing of Christian meanings on to old stories but the discerning of that prophetic and spiritual element which God has impressed upon these histories of the past, especially in all their climaxes and crises, when we see in the fact that God provided the ram which became the appointed sacrifice, through which Isaac's life was preserved, a dim adumbration of the great truth that the only Sacrifice which God accepts for the world's sin is the Sacrifice which He Himself has provided.

This is the deepest meaning of all the sacrificial worship, as of Israel so of heathen nations—God Himself will provide a Lamb. The world had built altars, and Israel, by divine appointment, had its altar too. All these express the want which none of them can satisfy. They show that man needed a Sacrifice and that Sacrifice God has provided. He asked from Abraham less than He gives to us. Abraham's devotion was sealed and certified because he did not withhold his son, his only son, from God. And God's love is sealed because He has not withheld His only-begotten Son from us.

So this name that came from Abraham's grateful and wondering lips contains a truth which holds true in all regions of our wants. On the lowest level, the outward supply of outward needs; on a higher, the means of discharging hard duties and a path through sharp trials; and, on the highest of all, the spotless sacrifice which alone avails for the world's sins—these are the things which God provides.

The Conditions in the Case

So, note again on what conditions He provides them.

The incident and the name became the occasion of a proverb, as the historian tells us, which survived down to the period of his writing, and probably long after, when men were accustomed to say, "In the mount of the Lord it shall be provided." The provision of all sorts that we need has certain conditions as to the when and the where of the persons to whom it shall be granted. "In the mount of the Lord it shall be provided." If we wish to have our outward needs supplied, our outward weaknesses strengthened, power and energy sufficient for duty, wisdom for perplexity, a share in the Sacrifice which takes away the sins of the world, we receive them all on the condition that we are found in the place where all God's provision is treasured. If a man chooses to sit outside the baker's shop, he may starve on its threshold. If a man will not go into the bank, his pockets will be empty though there may be bursting coffers there to which he has a right. And if we will not ascend to the hill of the Lord, and stand in His holy place by simple faith, and by true communion of heart and life, God's amplest provision is nought to us; and we are empty in the midst of affluence. Get near to God if you would partake of what He has prepared. Live in fellowship with Him by simple love and often meditate on Him if you would drink in of His fullness. And be sure of this, that howsoever within His house the stores are heaped and the treasury full, you will have neither part nor lot in the matter unless you are children of the house. "In the mount of the Lord it shall be provided." And round it there is a waste wilderness of famine and of death.

When the Provision Comes

Further, note *when* the provision is realized.

When the man is standing with the knife in his hand and the next minute it will be red with the son's blood—then the call comes: "Abraham!" and then he sees the ram caught in the thicket. There had been a long weary journey from their home away down in the dry, sunny south, a long tramp over the rough hills, a toilsome climb with a breaking heart in the father's bosom, and a dim foreboding gradually stealing on the child's spirit. But there was no sign of respite or of deliverance. Slowly he piles together the wood, and yet no sign. Slowly he binds his boy and lays him on it, and still no sign. Slowly, reluctantly, and yet resolvedly, he unsheathes the knife, and yet no sign. He lifts his hand, and then it comes.

That is God's way always. Up to the very edge we are driven before His hand is put out to help us. Such is the law, not only because the next moment is always necessarily dark nor because God will deal with us in any arbitrary fashion and play with our fears, but because it is best for us that we should be forced to desperation and out of desperation should "pluck the flower, safety." It is best for us that we should be brought to say, "My foot slippeth!" and then, just as our toes are sliding upon the glacier, the help comes and "Thy mercy held me up." "The Lord is our helper, and that right early." When He delays, it is not to trifle with us but to do us good by the sense of need as well as by the experience of deliverance. At the last moment, never before it, never until we have found out how much we need it, and never too late, comes the Helper.

So "it is provided" for the people that quietly and persistently tread the path of duty and go wherever His hand leads them without asking anything about where it does lead. The condition of the provision is our obedience of heart and will. To Abraham doing what he was commanded, though his heart was breaking as he did it, the help was granted—as it always will be.

What to Do with the Provision

And so, lastly, note what we are to do with the provision when we get it.

Abraham christened the anonymous mountaintop, not by a name that reminded him or others of his trial, but by a name that proclaimed God's deliverance. He did not say anything about his agony or about his obedience. God spoke about that, not Abraham. He did not want these to be remembered, but what he desired to hand on to later generations was what God had done for him. Oh! dear friends, is that the way in which we look back upon life? Many a bare, bald mountaintop in your career and mine we have names for. Are they names that commemorate our sufferings or God's blessings? When we look back on the past, what do we see? Times of trial or times of deliverance? Which side of the wave do we choose to look at, the one that is smitten by the sunshine or the one that is all black and purple in the shadow? The sea looked at from the one side will be all a sunny path, and from the other, dark as chaos. Let us name the heights that lie behind us, visible to memory, by names that commemorate, not the troubles that we had on them, but the deliverances that on them we received from God.

This name enshrines the duty of commemoration—yes! and the duty of expectation. "The Lord will provide." How do you know that, Abraham? And his answer is, "Because the Lord did provide." That is a shaky kind of argument if we use it about one another. Our resources may give out, our patience may weary. If it is a storehouse that we have to go to, all the corn that is treasured in it will be eaten up some day; but if it is to some boundless plain that grows it that we go, then we can be sure that there will be a harvest next year as there has been a harvest last.

And so we have to think of God not as a storehouse but as the soil from which there comes forth, year by year and generation after generation, the same crop of rich blessings for the needs and the hungers of every soul. If we have to draw from reservoirs we cannot say, "I have gone with my pitcher to the well six times, and I shall get it filled at the seventh." It is more probable that we shall have to say, "I have gone so often that I durst not go any more"; but if we have to go not to a well but to a fountain, then the oftener we go, the surer we become that its crystal cool waters will always be ready for us. "Thou hast been with me in six troubles; and in seven thou wilt not forsake me," is a bad conclusion to draw about one another; but it is the right conclusion to draw about God.

And so, as we look back upon our past lives and see many a peak gleaming in the magic light of memory, let us name them all by names that will throw a radiance of hope on the unknown and unclimbed difficulties before us and say, as the patriarch did when he went down from the mount of his trial and deliverance, "The Lord will provide."

NOTES

The Lord Our Righteousness

George Whitefield (1714-1770) was born in Gloucester, England, and educated at Pembroke College, Oxford. There he came under the influence of John and Charles Wesley, although Whitefield was more Calvinistic in doctrine than they. Ordained in the Anglican Church, he quickly gained a reputation as an effective preacher; but the Anglican churches disapproved of him because of his association with the Methodists. He began to preach to great crowds out of doors and led John Wesley to follow his example.

Whitefield made seven visits to America and is recognized as one of the leaders of evangelism and spiritual awakening in American history. This sermon is taken from *Memoirs of George Whitefield*, edited by John Gilles and published in 1837 by Hunt and Noyes. It is also found in *Select Sermons of George Whitefield*, published by Banner of Truth Trust.

George Whitefield

9

THE LORD OUR RIGHTEOUSNESS

Jeremiah 23:6

WHOEVER IS acquainted with the nature of mankind in general or the propensity of his own heart in particular must acknowledge that self-righteousness is the last idol that is rooted out of the heart. Being once born under a covenant of works, it is natural for us all to have recourse to a covenant of works for our everlasting salvation. And we have contracted such a devilish pride by our fall from God that we would, if not wholly yet in part at least, glory in being the cause of our own salvation. We cry out against Popery, and that very justly; but we are all Papists, at least I am sure we are all Arminians by nature; and, therefore, no wonder so many natural men embrace that scheme. It is true we disclaim the doctrine of merit and are ashamed directly to say we deserve any good at the hands of God; therefore, as the apostle excellently well observes, we go about establishing a righteousness of our own and, like the Pharisees of old, will not wholly submit to that righteousness which is of God, through Jesus Christ our Lord.

This is the sorest, though, alas! the most common evil that was ever yet seen under the sun, an evil that in any age, especially in these dregs of time wherein we live, cannot sufficiently be inveighed against. For as it is with the people, so it is with the priests; and it is to be feared even in those places where once the truth as it is in Jesus was eminently preached, many ministers are so sadly degenerated from their pious ancestors that the doctrines of grace, especially the personal, all-sufficient righteousness of Jesus, are but too seldom, too slightly mentioned. Hence the love of many waxeth cold; and I have often thought, was it possible that this single consideration would be sufficient to raise our venerable forefathers again from their graves who would thunder in their ears their fatal error.

The righteousness of Jesus Christ is one of those great mysteries which the angels desire to *look into* and seems to be one of the first lessons that God taught men after the fall. For what were the coats that God made to put on our first parents but types of the application of the merits of righteousness of Jesus Christ to believers' hearts? We are told that those coats were made of skins of beasts; and as beasts were not then food for men, we may fairly infer that those beasts were slain in sacrifice, in commemoration of the great sacrifice, Jesus Christ, thereafter to be offered. And the skins of those beasts thus slain, being put on Adam and Eve, they were thereby taught how their nakedness was to be covered with the righteousness of the Lamb of God.

This is it which is meant when we are told Abraham believed on the Lord, and it was counted to him for righteousness. In short, this is it of which both the law and all the prophets have spoken, especially Jeremiah in the words of the text: *The Lord our righteousness.*

I propose, through divine grace:

I. To consider *who* we are to understand by the word *Lord.*
II. *How* the *Lord* is man's righteousness.
III. I will consider some of the *chief objections* that are generally urged against *this* doctrine.
IV. I shall show some very *ill consequences* that flow naturally from *denying* this doctrine.
V. I shall conclude with an exhortation to *all* to *come to Christ by faith,* that they may be enabled to say with the prophet in the text, *The Lord our righteousness.*

Who

First, I am to consider who we are to understand by the word *Lord—The Lord our righteousness.*

And if any Arians or Socinians are drawn by curiosity to hear what the babbler has to say, let them be ashamed of denying the divinity of that Lord that has bought poor sinners with His precious blood. For the person mentioned in the text under the character of *Lord*, is Jesus Christ. "*Behold* (v. 5), *the days come, saith the Lord, that I will raise unto David a righteous branch, a King shall reign and prosper, shall execute judgment and justice in the earth. In his day* (v. 6), *Judah shall be saved, and Israel shall dwell safely; and this is his name whereby he shall be called, The Lord our righteousness.*" By the *righteous Branch*, all agree that we are to understand Jesus Christ. He it is Who is called the Lord in our text. If so, if there were no other text in the Bible to prove the divinity of Christ, that is sufficient. For if the word *Lord* may properly belong to Jesus Christ, He must be God. For as you have it in the margins of your Bibles, the word *Lord* is in the original *Jehovah* which is the essential title of God Himself. Come, then, ye Arians, kiss the Son of God, bow down before Him, and honor Him even as you honor the Father. Learn of the angels, those morning stars, and worship Him as truly God. For otherwise you are as much idolaters as those who worship the Virgin Mary. And as for you, Socinians, who say Christ was a mere man and yet profess that He was your Savior, according to your own principles, you are accursed. For, if Christ be a mere man, then He is only an arm of flesh. And it is written, *Cursed is he that trusteth on an arm of flesh.* But I would hope there are no such monsters here. At least, that after these considerations, they would be ashamed of broaching such monstrous absurdities anymore. For it is plain that by the word Lord, we are to understand the Lord Jesus Christ who here takes to Himself the title of *Jehovah* and therefore must be very God of very God, or, as the apostle devoutly expresses it, God *blessed forevermore.*

How

How the Lord is to be *man's righteousness* comes next to be considered.

And that is, in one word, by *imputation.* For it pleased God, after He had made all things *by the word of His power*, to create man after His own image. And so infinite was the condescension of the high and lofty One, Who inhabiteth eternity, that although He might have insisted on the everlasting obedience of him and his posterity, yet He was pleased to oblige Himself by a covenant or agreement made with His own creatures upon condition of an unsinning obedience, to give them immortality and eternal life. For when it is said, *the day that thou eatest thereof thou shalt surely die,* we may fairly infer so long as he continued obedient and did not eat thereof, he should surely live. Genesis 3 gives us a full but mournful account how our first parents broke this covenant and thereby stood in need of a better righteousness than their own in order to procure their future acceptance with God. For what must they do? They were as much under a covenant of works as ever. And, though after their disobedience they were without strength, yet they were obliged not only to do but continue to do all things, and that too in the most perfect manner which the Lord had required of them, and not only so, but to make satisfaction to God's infinitely offended justice for the breach of which they had already been guilty.

Here then opens the amazing scene of divine philanthropy; I mean, God's love to man. For behold, what man could not do, Jesus Christ, the Son of the Father's love, undertakes to do for him. And that God might be just in justifying the ungodly though He was in the form of God and therefore thought it no robbery to be equal with God, yet He took upon Him the form of a servant, even human nature. In that nature He obeyed, and thereby fulfilled the whole moral law in our stead, and also died a painful death upon the cross, and thereby became a curse for, or instead of, those whom the Father had given Him. As God, He satisfied at the same time that He obeyed and suffered as man; and being God and man in one person, wrought out a full, perfect, and sufficient righteousness for all to whom it was to be imputed.

Here then we see the meaning of the word *righteousness.* It implies the active as well as passive obedience of the Lord Jesus Christ. Generally, when talking of the merits of Christ, we only mention the latter, i.e., His death;

whereas the former, i.e., His life and active obedience, is equally necessary. Christ is not such a Savior as becomes us unless we join both together. Christ not only died but lived; not only suffered but obeyed, for or instead of poor sinners. And both these jointly make up that complete righteousness which is to be imputed to us as the disobedience of our first parents was made ours by *imputation*. In this sense and no other are we to understand that parallel which St. Paul draws in Romans 5 between the first and second Adam. This is what he elsewhere terms our *being made the righteousness of God in Him*. This is the sense wherein the prophet would have us understand the words of the text; therefore, Jeremiah 16, *She*, i.e., the church itself shall be called (having this righteousness imputed to her) the *Lord our righteousness*. A passage, I think, worthy of the profoundest meditation of all the sons and daughters of Adam.

Objections

Many are the objections which the proud hearts of fallen men are continually urging against this wholesome, this divine, this soul-saving doctrine. I come now, in the third place, to answer some few of those which I think the most considerable.

And first, they say, because they would appear friends to morality, "That the doctrine of an imputed righteousness is destructive of good works, and leads to licentiousness."

And who, pray, are the persons who generally urge this objection? Are they men full of faith, and men really concerned for good works? No, whatever few exceptions there may be if there be any at all, it is notorious, they are generally men of corrupt minds, reprobate concerning the faith. The best title I can give them is that of profane moralists or moralists falsely so called. For I appeal to the experience of the present as well as past ages if iniquity did and does not most abound where the doctrine of Christ's whole personal righteousness is most cried down and most seldom mentioned. Arminian being anti-Christian principles always did and always will lead to anti-

Christian practices. And never was there a reformation brought about in the church but by preaching the doctrine of Christ's imputed righteousness. This, as that man of God, Luther, calls it, is *Articulus stantis aut cadentis Ecclesia*, the article upon which the church stands or falls. And though the preachers of this doctrine are generally branded by those on the other side with the opprobrious names of Antinomians, deceivers, and what not; yet, I believe if the truth of the doctrine on both sides were to be judged of by the lives of the preachers and professors of it, those on our side of the question would have the advantage every way.

It is true, this, as well as every other doctrine of grace, may be abused. And perhaps the unChristian walk of some who have talked of Christ's imputed righteousness, justification by faith, and the life, and yet never felt it imputed to their own souls has given the enemies of the Lord thus cause to blaspheme. But this is a very unsafe as well as very unfair way of arguing. The only question should be, Whether or not this doctrine of an imputed righteousness does, in itself, cut off the occasion of good works or lead to licentiousness? No, in no wise. It excludes works indeed from being any cause of our justification in the sight of God. But it requires good works as a proof of our having this righteousness imputed to us and as a declarative evidence of our justification in the sight of men. And then how can the doctrine of an imputed righteousness be a doctrine leading to licentiousness?

It is all calumny. St. Paul introduces an infidel making this objection in his epistle to the Romans. And none but infidels, who never felt the power of Christ's resurrection upon the souls, will urge it over again. And therefore, notwithstanding this objection, with the prophet in the text we may boldly say, *The Lord our righteousness.*

But Satan (and no wonder that his servants imitate him) often *transforms himself into an angel of light.* And therefore (such perverse things will infidelity and Arminianism make men speak), in order to dress their objections in the best colors, some urge "that our Savior preached no such doctrine—that in His sermon upon the mount, He mentions only morality," and consequently the doctrine of an imputed righteousness falls wholly to the ground.

But surely the men who urge this objection either never read or never understood our blessed Lord's discourse wherein the doctrine of an imputed righteousness is so plainly taught that he who runs, if he has eyes that see, may read.

Indeed our Lord does recommend morality and good works (as all faithful ministers will do) and clears the moral law from the many corrupt glosses put upon it by the letter-learned Pharisees. But then, before He comes to this, it is remarkable, He talks of inward piety such as poverty of spirit, meekness, holy mourning, purity of heart, especially hungering and thirsting after righteousness, and then recommends good works as an evidence of our having His righteousness imputed to us and these graces and divine tempers wrought in our hearts. "Let your light (that is, the divine light I before have been mentioning), shine before men, in a holy life, that they, seeing your good works, may glorify your Father which is in heaven." And then immediately adds, "Think not that I am come to destroy the *moral law*—I came not to destroy, to take away the force of it as a rule of life, but to fulfill, to obey it in its whole latitude, and give the complete sense of it." And then He goes on to show how exceeding broad the moral law is so that our Lord, instead of disannulling an imputed righteousness in His sermon upon the mount, not only confirms it, but also answers the foregoing objection urged against it by making good works a proof and evidence of its being imputed to our souls. He, therefore, who has ears to hear, let him hear what the prophet says in the words of the text—*The Lord our righteousness*.

But as Satan not only quoted Scripture but also backed one temptation with it after another when he attacked Christ's person in the wilderness, so His children generally take the same method in treating His doctrine. And therefore they urge another objection against the doctrine of an imputed righteousness from the example of the young man in the gospel.

We may state it thus: "The evangelist, St. Mark," say

they, "chapter 10, mentions a young man who came to Christ, running and asking Him what he should do to inherit eternal life? Christ, say they, referred him to the commandments to know what he must do to inherit eternal life. It is plain, therefore, works were to be partly, at least, the cause of his justification; and consequently the doctrine of an imputed righteousness is unscriptural." This is the objection in its full strength; and little strength is in all its fullness. For, were I to prove the necessity of an imputed righteousness, I scarce know how I could bring a better instance to make it good.

Let us take a more intimate view of this young man and our Lord's behavior toward him. In Mark 10:17, the evangelist tells us, "That when Christ was gone forth into the way, there came one running (it should seem it was some nobleman, a rarity indeed, to see such a one running to Christ!) and not only so, but he kneeled to Him (though many of his rank scarce know the time when they kneeled to Christ), and *asked Him, saying, 'Good Master what shall I do that I may inherit eternal life?'* Then Jesus, to see whether or not he believed Him to be what He really was, truly and properly God, said unto him, *'Why callest thou me good? there is none good but one, that is God.'* And that He might directly answer his question; says He, *'Thou knowest the commandments: Do not commit adultery, Do not bear false witness, Defraud not, Honor thy father and thy mother.'*" This, I say, was a direct answer to his question; namely, that eternal life was not to be attained by his doings. For our Lord, by referring him to the commandments, did not (as the objectors insinuate), in the least, hint that his morality would recommend him to the favor and mercy of God. But He intended thereby to make the law His schoolmaster to bring him to Himself that the young man, seeing how he had broken every one of these commandments, might thereby be convinced of the insufficiency of his own, and consequently of the absolute necessity of looking out for a better righteousness, whereon he might depend for eternal life.

This was what our Lord designed. The young man,

being self-righteous and willing to justify himself, said, *"All these have I observed from my youth."* But had he known himself, he would have confessed, *"All these have I broken from my youth."* For supposing he had not actually committed adultery, had he never lusted after a woman in his heart? What if he had not really killed another, had he never been angry without a cause or spoken unadvisedly with his lips? If so, by breaking one of the least commandments in the least degree, he became liable to the curse of God: For *"cursed is he* (saith the law) *that continueth not to do all things that are written in this book."* And therefore, as I observed before, our Lord was so far from speaking against this that He treated the young man in that manner on purpose to convince him of the necessity of an imputed righteousness.

But perhaps they will reply, it is said, *Jesus beholding him, loved him.* And what then? This He might do with a human love, and at the same time this young man have no interest in His blood. Thus Christ is said to wonder, to weep over Jerusalem, and say, *Oh that thou hadst* KNOWN, etc. But such like passages are to be referred only to His human nature. And there is a great deal of difference between the love wherewith Christ loved this young man and that wherewith He loved Mary, Lazarus, and their sister Martha. To illustrate this by a comparison: A minister of the Lord Jesus Christ, seeing many amiable dispositions such as a readiness to hear the Word, a decent behavior at public worship, a life outwardly spotless in many, cannot but so far love them. But then there is much difference between that love which a minister feels for such and that divine love, that union and sympathy of soul, which he feels for those that he is satisfied are really born again of God. Apply this to our Lord's case as a faint illustration of it. Consider what has been said upon the young man's case in general; and then, if before you were fond of this objection, instead of triumphing like him, you will go sorrowful away. Our Savior's reply to him more and more convinces us of the truth of the prophet's assertion in the text, i.e., that *the Lord is our righteousness.*

But there is a fourth and grand objection yet behind,

and that is taken from Matthew 25, "where our Lord is described, as rewarding people with eternal life, because they fed the hungry, clothed the naked, and such like. Their works therefore were a cause of their justification; consequently, the doctrine of imputed righteousness is not agreeable to Scripture."

This, I confess, is the most plausible objection brought against the doctrine insisted on from the text. And in order that we may answer it in as clear and as brief a manner as may be, we confess, with the article of the Church of England, "That albeit good works do not justify us, yet they will follow after justification, as fruits of it; and though they can claim no reward in themselves, yet forasmuch as they spring from faith in Christ, and a renewed soul, they shall receive a reward *of grace*, though not *of debt*; and consequently, the more we abound in such good works, the greater will be our reward when Jesus Christ shall come to judgment."

Take considerations along with us, and they will help us much to answer the objection now before us. For thus does Matthew say: *"Then shall the King say to them on his right hand, Come ye blessed children of my Father, inherit the kingdom prepared for you from the foundation of the world.—For I was an hungered, and ye gave me meat. I was thirsty, and ye gave me drink. I was a stranger, and ye took me in. Naked, and ye clothed me. I was sick, and ye visited me. I was in prison, and ye came unto me."* "I will therefore reward you, because you have done these things out of love to me, and hereby have evidenced yourselves to be my true disciples." And that the people did not depend on these good actions for their justification in the sight of God is evident. *"For when saw we thee an hungered,"* say they, *"and fed thee? Or thirsty, and gave thee drink? When saw we thee a stranger, and took thee in? Or naked, and clothed thee? Or when saw we thee sick, or in prison, and came unto thee?"*—Language and questions quite improper for persons relying on their own righteousness for acceptance in the sight of God.

But then they reply against this. In the latter part of the chapter, say they, it is plain that Jesus Christ rejects and damns the others for not doing these things. And therefore, if He damns those for not doing, He saves those for doing; and consequently the doctrine of an imputed righteousness is good for nothing.

But that is no consequence at all—For God may justly damn any man for omitting the least duty of the moral law, and yet in Himself He is not obliged to give any one any reward, supposing he has done all that he can. We are unprofitable servants, we have done not near so much as it was our duty to do must be the language of the most holy souls living; and therefore from or in ourselves, we cannot be justified in the sight of God. This was the frame of the devout souls just referred to. Sensible of this, they were so far from depending on their works for justification in the sight of God that they were filled, as it were with a holy blushing, to think our Lord should condescend to mention, much more to reward them for their poor works of faith and labors of love. I am persuaded their hearts would rise with a holy indignation against those who urge this passage as an objection against the assertion of the prophet in the words of the text, that the *Lord is our righteousness.*

Thus I think we have fairly answered these grand objections which are generally urged against the doctrine of an imputed righteousness. Were I to stop here, I think I might say we are made more than conquerors through Him that loved us. But there is a way of arguing which I have always admired because I have thought it always very convincing, i.e., by showing the absurdities that will follow from denying any particular proposition in dispute.

The Consequences of Denial

This is the fourth thing that was proposed. "And never did greater or more absurdities flow from the denying any doctrine, than will flow from denying the doctrine of Christ's imputed righteousness."

And first, if we deny this doctrine, we turn the truth, I mean the Word of God, as much as we can into a lie and utterly subvert all those places of Scripture which say, *That we are saved by grace; that it is not of works, lest any man should boast.* That salvation is God's free gift—and that *He that glorieth, must glory only in the Lord.* For, if the whole personal righteousness of Jesus Christ be not the sole cause of my acceptance with God, if any work done by or foreseen in me was in the least to be joined with it or looked upon by God as an inducing, impulsive cause of acquitting my soul from guilt, then I have somewhat whereof I may glory in myself. Now boasting is excluded in the great work of our redemption. But that cannot be if we are enemies to the doctrine of an imputed righteousness. It would be endless to enumerate how many texts of Scripture must be false if this doctrine be not true. Let it suffice to affirm in the general that if we deny an imputed righteousness, we may as well deny a divine revelation all at once. For it is the Alpha and Omega, the beginning and the end of the book of God. We must either disbelieve that or believe what the prophet has spoken in the text, *That the Lord is our righteousness.*

But farther—I observed at the beginning of this discourse that we are all Arminians and Papists by nature; for, as one observes, Arminianism is the back way to Popery. And here I venture further to affirm, "that if we deny the doctrine of an imputed righteousness, whatever we may style ourselves, we are really Papists in our hearts, and deserve no other title from men."

Sirs, what think you? Suppose I were to come and tell you that you must intercede with saints for them to intercede with God for you. Would you not then say I was justly reputed a Popish missionary by some and deservedly thrust out of the synagogues by others? I suppose you would. And why? Because you would say the intercession of Jesus Christ was sufficient of itself without the intercession of saints; and that it was blasphemous to join theirs with His as though it was not sufficient.

Suppose I went a little more round about and told you that the death of Christ was not sufficient without our death being added to it; that you must die as well as Christ, join your death with His, and then it would be sufficient. Might you not then with a holy indignation throw dust in the air and justly call me a setter forth of strange doctrines? And now then, if it be not only absurd but blasphemous to join the intercession of saints with the intercession of Christ as though His intercession was not sufficient, or our death with the death of Christ as though His death was not sufficient, judge ye, if it be not equally absurd, equally blasphemous, to join our obedience either wholly or in part with the obedience of Christ as if that was not sufficient. And if so, what absurdities will follow the denying that the Lord, both as to His active and passive obedience, is our righteousness?

One more absurdity I shall mention that will follow from the denying this doctrine, and I have done.

I remember a story of a certain prelate, who, after many arguments in vain urged to convince the Earl of Rochester of the invisible realities of another world, took his leave of his lordship with some such words as these: "Well my lord," says he, "if there be no hell, I am safe; but if there be such a thing, my lord, as hell, what will become of you?" I apply this to those who oppose the doctrine not insisted on. If there be no such thing as the doctrine of an imputed righteousness, those who hold it, and bring forth fruit unto holiness, are safe. But if there be such a thing (as there certainly is), what will become of you who deny it? It is no difficult matter to determine. Your portion must be in the lake of fire and brimstone forever and ever; since you will rely upon your works, by your works you shall be judged. They shall be weighed in the balance of the sanctuary. They will be found wanting. By your works, therefore, shall you be condemned; and you, being out of Christ, shall find God, to your poor wretched souls, a consuming fire.

The great Stoddard, of Northampton, in New England, has therefore well entitled a book which he wrote (and which I would take this opportunity to recommend), *The Safety of Appearing in the Righteousness of Christ*. For why should I lean upon a broken reed when I can have the Rock of Ages to stand upon that never can be moved?

And now, before I come to a more particular application, give me leave, in the apostle's language, triumphantly to cry out, Where is the scribe? Where the disputer? Where is the reasoning infidel of this generation? Can anything appear more reasonable, even according to your own way of arguing, than the doctrine here laid down? Have you not felt a convincing power go along with the word? Why then will you not believe on the Lord Jesus Christ so that He may become the Lord your righteousness.

But it is time to come a little closer to your consciences.

Brethren, though some may be offended at this doctrine and may account it foolishness, yet to many of you I doubt not but it is precious, it being agreeable to the form of sound words which from your infancy has been delivered to you; and coming from a quarter you would least have expected, may be received with more pleasure and satisfaction. But give me leave to ask you one question, Can you say, the Lord our righteousness? I say, the Lord our righteousness. For entertaining this doctrine in your heads, without receiving the Lord Jesus Christ savingly by a lively faith into your hearts, will but increase your damnation. As I have often told you, so I tell you again, an unapplied Christ is no Christ at all.

Can you then, with believing Thomas, cry out, *My Lord, and my God*? Is Christ your sanctification, as well as your outward righteousness? For the word righteousness in the text not only implies Christ's personal righteousness imputed to us but also holiness of heart wrought in us. These two God has joined together. He never did, He never does, He never will put them asunder. If you are justified by the *blood*, you are also sanctified by the Spirit of the Lord. Can you then in this sense say, the Lord our righteousness? Were you never made to abhor yourselves for your actual and original sins and to loathe your own righteousness (or, as the prophet beautifully expresses it, your righteousnesses), as filthy rags? Were you never made to see and admire the all-sufficiency of Christ's righteousness and excited by the Spirit of God be athirst for Christ, yes, even for the righteousness of Christ?

O when shall I come to appear before the presence of my God in the righteousness of Christ! O nothing but Christ! Nothing but Christ! Give me Christ, O God, and I am satisfied! My soul shall praise Thee forever. Was this,

I say, ever the language of your hearts? And after these inward conflicts, were you ever enabled to reach out the arm of faith and embrace the blessed Jesus in your souls so that you could say, *My beloved is mine, and I am his?* If so, fear not, whoever you are. Hail, all hail, you happy souls! The Lord, the Lord Christ, the everlasting God is your righteousness. Christ has justified you, who is he that condemneth you?

Christ has died for you, nay rather is risen again, and ever liveth to make intercession for you. Being now justified by His grace, you have peace with God and shall before long be with Jesus in glory, reaping everlasting and unspeakable redemption both in body and soul for there is no condemnation to those who are really in Christ Jesus. Whether Paul or Apollos, or life or death, all is yours if you are Christ's, for Christ is God's! O my brethren, my heart is enlarged toward you! O, think on the love of Christ in dying for you! If the Lord be your righteousness, let the righteousness of your Lord be continually in your mouth. Talk of, oh talk of and recommend the righteousness of Christ, when you lie down and when you rise up, at your going out and coming in! Think of the greatness of the gift as well as the giver! Show to all the world in whom you have believed! Let all, by your fruits, know that the Lord is your righteousness and that you are waiting for your Lord from heaven!

O study to be holy, even as He Who has called you and washed you in His own blood is holy! Let not the righteousness of the Lord be evil spoken of through you. Let not Jesus be wounded in the house of His friends; but grow in grace and in the knowledge of our Lord and Savior Jesus Christ day by day. O, think of His dying love! Let that love constrain you to obedience. Having much forgiven, love much. Be always asking, What shall I do to express my gratitude to the Lord for giving me His righteousness? Let that self-abasing, God-exalting question be always in your mouths. O be always lisping out, Why me, Lord? Why me? Why am I taken and others left? Why is the Lord my righteousness? Why is He become my salvation, who have so often deserved damnation at His hands?

An Exhortation

O, my friends, I trust I feel somewhat of a sense of God's distinguishing love upon my heart! Therefore I must divert a little from congratulating you, to invite poor Christless sinners to come to Him and accept of His righteousness that they may have life.

Alas, my heart almost bleeds! What a multitude of precious souls are now before me! How shortly must all be ushered into eternity; and yet, O cutting thought! was God now to require all your souls, how few, comparatively speaking, could really say, *the Lord our righteousness.*

And think you, O sinners, that you will be able to stand in the day of judgment if Christ be not your righteousness? No, that alone is the wedding garment in which you must appear. O, Christless sinners, I am distressed for you! The desires of my soul are enlarged! O, that this may be an accepted time! O, that the Lord may be your righteousness! For whither would you flee if death should find you naked? Indeed there is no hiding yourselves from His presence. The pitiful fig leaves of your own righteousness will not cover your nakedness when God shall call you to stand before Him. Adam found them ineffectual, and so will you.

O, think of death! O, think of judgment! Yet a little while and time shall be no more; and then what will become of you if the Lord be not your righteousness? Think you that Christ will spare you? No, He Who formed you will have no mercy on you. If you are out of Christ, if Christ be not your righteousness, Christ Himself will pronounce you damned. And can you bear to think of being damned by Christ? Can you bear to hear the Lord Jesus say unto you, *"Depart from me, ye cursed, into everlasting life, prepared for the devil and his angels"*? Can you live, think you, in everlasting burnings? Is your flesh brass and your bones iron? What if they are? Hell fire, that fire prepared for the devil and his angels, will heat them through and through!

And can you bear to depart from Christ? O, that heart-piercing thought! Ask those holy souls who are at any time bewailing absent God, who walk in darkness and see no light though but a few days or hours; ask them, what it is to lose a sight and presence of Christ? See how they seek Him sorrowing and go mourning after Him all the day long! And if it is so dreadful to lose the sensible presence of Christ only for a day, what must it be to be banished from Him to all eternity? But thus it must be if Christ be not your righteousness. For God's justice must be satisfied; and unless Christ's righteousness is imputed and applied to you here, you must be satisfying the divine justice in hell torments eternally, hereafter.

Nay, as I said before, Christ Himself, the God of love, shall condemn you to that place of torment. And O, how cutting is that thought! Methinks I see poor, trembling, Christless wretches, standing before the bar of God, crying out, "Lord, if we must be damned, let some angel, or some archangel, pronounce the damnatory sentence." But all in vain. Christ Himself shall pronounce the irrevocable sentence. Knowing, therefore, the terrors of the Lord, let me persuade you to close with Christ and never rest, till you can say, "The Lord our righteousness." Who knows but the Lord may have mercy on, nay, abundantly pardon you? Beg of God to give you faith; and if the Lord give you that, you will by it receive Christ with His righteousness and His all.

You need not fear the greatness or number of your sins. For are you sinners? So am I. Are you the chief of sinners? So am I. Are you backsliding sinners? So am I. And yet the Lord (forever adored be His rich, free, and sovereign grace), the Lord is my righteousness. Come, then, O young men, who (as I acted once myself) are playing the prodigal and wandering away afar off from your swine's trough—feed no longer on the husks of sensual delights. For Christ's sake, arise and come home! Your heavenly Father now calls you. See it, view it again and again. Consider at how dear a rate it was purchased, even by the blood of God. Consider what great need you have of it. You are lost, undone, damned forever, without it.

Come then, poor, guilty prodigals, come home. Indeed I will not, like the elder brother, be angry. No, I will rejoice with the angels in heaven. And, that God would now bow the heavens and come down! "Descend, O Son of God, descend; and as thou hast shown in me such mercy, O let the blessed Spirit apply thy righteousness to some prodigals now before Thee and clothe their naked souls with Thy best robe."

But I must speak a word to you, young maidens, as well as young men. I see many of you adorned as to your bodies; but are not your souls naked! Which of you can say, the Lord is my righteousness? Which of you was ever solicitous to be dressed in this robe of invaluable price, and without which you are no better than whited sepulchers in the sight of God? Let not then so many of you, young maidens, any longer forget your only ornament: Oh, seek for the Lord to be your righteousness or otherwise burning will soon be upon you instead of beauty!

And what shall I say to you of a middle age, you busy merchants, you cumbered Marthas, who with all your gettings, have not yet gotten the Lord to be your righteousness? Alas! what profit will there be of all your labor under the sun if you do not secure this pearl of invaluable price? This one thing, so absolutely needful, that it can only stand you instead when all other things shall be taken from you. Labor therefore no longer so anxiously for the meat which perisheth, but henceforward seek for the Lord to be your righteousness, a righteousness that will entitle you to life everlasting.

I see also many gray heads here, and perhaps the most of them cannot say, the Lord is my righteousness. O gray-headed sinners, I could weep over you! Your gray hairs which ought to be your crown, and in which perhaps you glory, are now your shame. You know not that the Lord is your righteousness. Oh, haste then, haste, ye aged sinners, and seek an interest in redeeming love!

Alas, you have one foot already in the grave. Your glass is just run out. Your sun is just going down, and it will set and leave you in an eternal darkness unless the Lord be your righteousness! Flee then, oh, flee for your lives! Be not afraid. All things are possible with God. If you come, though it be at the eleventh hour, Christ Jesus will in nowise cast you out. Oh, seek then for the Lord to be your righteousness, and beseech Him to let you know how it is that a man may be born again when he is old!

But I must not forget the lambs of the flock. To feed them was one of my Lord's last commands; I know He will be angry with me if I do not tell them that the Lord may be their righteousness and that of such is the kingdom of heaven. Come then, you little children, come to Christ; the Lord Christ shall be your righteousness. Do not think that you are too young to be converted. Perhaps many of you may be nine or ten years old and yet cannot say the Lord is our righteousness which many have said, though younger than you. Come then, while you are young. Perhaps you may not live to be old. Do not wait for other people. If your fathers and mothers will not come to Christ, do you come without them. Let children lead them and show them how the Lord may be their righteousness. Our Lord Jesus loved little children. You are His lambs. He bids me feed you. I pray God make you willing betimes to take the Lord for your righteousness.

Did you never read of the Eunuch belonging to the queen of Candace? He believed—The Lord was his righteousness, he was baptized. Do you also believe, and you shall be saved. Christ Jesus is the same now as He was yesterday and will wash you in His own blood. Go home then, turn the words of the text into a prayer, and entreat the Lord to be your righteousness. *Even so, come Lord Jesus, come quickly*, into all our souls! *Amen*, Lord Jesus, *Amen* and *Amen*.

The Strength of the Name

George Campbell Morgan (1863-1945) was the son of a British Baptist preacher and preached his first sermon when he was 13 years old. He had no formal training for the ministry, but his tireless devotion to the study of the Bible helped him to become one of the leading Bible teachers of his day. Rejected by the Methodists, he was ordained into the Congregational ministry. He was associated with Dwight L. Moody in the Northfield Bible conferences and as an itinerant Bible teacher. He is best known as the pastor of the Westminster Chapel, London (1904-17 and 1933-45). During his second term there, he had Dr. D. Martyn Lloyd-Jones as his associate.

Morgan published more than 60 books and booklets, and his sermons are found in *The Westminster Pulpit* (London, Pickering and Inglis). This sermon is from Volume 4. While it is not on a specific name of God, it applies the meaning of "the name of the Lord" to practical life, and particularly in the second section which deals with several of the names of God.

George Campbell Morgan

10

THE STRENGTH OF THE NAME

The name of Jehovah is a strong tower: The righteous runneth into it, and is safe (Proverbs 18:10).

LIFE IS FULL of strain and stress. Sooner or later we all come to the consciousness of this fact. The illustrative figures of the inspired Scriptures all remind us of this fact.

Life is described as a race for the running of which it is necessary that we should lay aside all weights, and forgetting the things we pass as soon as they are passed, with eyes earnestly fixed upon the goal, so run that we may obtain.

Or life is described as a voyage, and the suggestion is that of the need the mariner has for skill and constant watchfulness that he may escape the perils of rocks and sand-banks and shoals.

Or life is described as a battle in which the warrior must be fully panoplied and prepared to stand and to withstand in order that, having done all, he may stand.

Or life is considered as a great problem, full of perplexity in which every day brings its new amazement, all the way is a way in which the pilgrim passes through mystery and into mystery.

All these figures suggest the strain and stress of life.

There come to every one of us, sooner or later, days when strength is weakened. These are the days of disaster or victory in human life, the days in which we find that of ourselves and in ourselves we are unequal to navigating the vessel, to prosecuting the battle to finality, to discovering the way along which we should walk, and to continuing therein in spite of difficulty. The day when we have to say *we cannot* is a day of disaster or a day of victory and whether it be disaster or victory depends en-

tirely upon whether or not we believe our text and have
entered into the full meaning of its profound and comfort-
ing suggestiveness. "The name of Jehovah is a strong
tower: The righteous runneth into it, and is set on high."

The Forces Against Us

Let us first remind ourselves of the forces that are
against us in order that we may then consider what this
text suggests as to the place of safety in order that we
may finally consider the proofs of safety.

Of the forces that have been and still are against us,
the first are mystic and strange and not perfectly understood; they are spiritual antagonisms. We have been conscious in the midst of life of the sudden assaults of evil.
We deny absolutely that they came from within. They
were not part of ourselves. We do not believe that they
came from God, but we are quite sure of the assault. Over
and over again we are made conscious, whatever our philosophy may be, that there are spiritual forces, insidious
and subtle, which suggest evil; and we are appalled by
the overwhelming strength of these spiritual antagonisms.

Or, to speak of these things as they are personified, we
are perpetually antagonized by one who has been described
as "seeking whom he may devour," one who finds his way,
if Scripture be true, into the immediate presence of God,
there to slander and to ask permission to test us that he
may sift us as wheat. The revelation of the antagonism of
this evil spirit flames into supreme revelation in the Book
of Job, and especially in one very remarkable sentence in
that Book where it is said that God inquires of him, "Hast
thou *considered* My servant Job?" "Hast thou *considered?*"
The question reveals an enemy who is patiently watching—watching for the weakest place in the chain that
there he may attempt to break it; watching for the least
guarded door in the citadel of man-soul that there he may
force an entrance.

But there are other forces against us. The age in which
we live is full of things that hinder us in our attempt to
live the godly life. Let me name one or two of them. First,
there is the fact that men are so eminently successful

without God. That may sound a strange thing to say. The preacher is always denying it, and there is a sense in which we shall still continue to deny it. But it is impossible for the man of business, who is attempting to be a godly man, to look out upon his age without seeing how marvelously well men seem to get on without God.

Or, there is the problem of the long continued victory of evil in the world, the fact that time after time when it seems as though morning were breaking, it suddenly darkens into midnight.

Then there is the problem of universal pain, the problem that floods me with letters which I am always in amazed difficulty as to how to answer.

These are among the things that make life strenuous, and create the sense of strain, and demand some place of quietness and some place of peace.

Or, again, we have to do with the persistence of the self-life. I often feel that the enemy I dread most is not the devil, not the problems by which I am surrounded, but myself. The reappearance of the self-life is perpetual. Immediately a man thinks he has gained a victory over it, mastered it, it garbs itself in other vestments and appears anew.

And then, there are the sorrows of life, the bereavements that come to us, the empty places in the home, the hope deferred that makes the heart sick, the disappointments that crush the spirit in personal friendships, the hour in which a man has to say:

> Yea, mine own familiar friend, in whom I trusted, which did eat my bread,
> Hath lifted up his heel against me.

These are some of the forces against us. Individually they defeat us; united they destroy us.

The Place of Safety

Now what are we to do? It is in the midst of a Book that is full of the revelation of these contrary forces, a Book that recognizes the spiritual antagonisms, that this wonderful verse flames out. It seems to be very much alone in this chapter of Proverbs. Yet, there is a wonderful fitness that this verse is put down into the midst of words that seem to have no connection with it. Into the chaos it comes with its suggestion of cosmos, into the darkness with its flaming light, into a sob and a sigh with its song. "The name of Jehovah is a strong tower: The righteous runneth into it, and is safe."

Let us attempt to interpret the meaning of this text by the Book because the name of Jehovah is related to the whole of the old economy. I pray you remember the use these Hebrew people made of that name, the fact that they never pronounced it as we pronounce it, the fact that they never wrote it in fullness so that they have created for us unto this hour a difficulty as to what the full name really was. On all the pages of their ancient Scriptures this particular name, to which the preacher now refers, stands revealed by four consonants with no vowels, indicating a reverent reticence in the pronunciation of a name so full of rich suggestiveness. And remember, moreover, that as you study these Old Testament Scriptures, you never find this name linked with any qualifying or distinguishing adjective. You never read, *the* Jehovah, or *my* Jehovah, or *the living* Jehovah. The Adonai, the Lord; my Elohim, my God; the living Elohim, the living God; but never the, my, or the living Jehovah. It always stands alone as the tetragrammaton, four consonants from which the light seems to break. There was a singular reverence and reticence in the use of the name, and yet, it was the very center of the Hebrew religion; and the measure in which these people rose to any height of religious life was the measure in which they saw the light of that name, and took their refuge in its signification, and were made strong by all it said to them.

I know the difficulty of interpretation, but I do not hesitate to adopt the interpretation that it means the Becoming One—that is, the One Who becomes to His people all they need. It suggests the adaptation of Infinite Being to finite being in order to bring about the strengthening of finite being with all the strength of Infinite Being. If it is difficult to follow that line and to discover the mystery of the tetragrammaton, then let us turn to the name as it is illustrated for us in the Old Testament in five pictures.

The first is that of Abraham on a mountain with Isaac. The second is of Moses on a mountain. In the valley are the hosts that he has led from Egypt's slavery engaged in deadly conflict with Amalek. Moses' hands are lifted in prayer, and while they are so lifted Israel prevails, and when they faint and droop Amalek prevails. The third is the picture of Gideon, the peaceful farmer, suddenly called to national service, commanded to gather an army and to strike a blow that shall break the power of Midian. The fourth is a picture of a prophet in prison—Jeremiah, exercising a ministry in which there is no gleam of hope as to immediate result; knowing this from the commencement until at last he is in prison, and in the prison house he is singing a song of hope. And the last is the picture of yet another prophet, an exile from his own land by the River Chebar—Ezekiel, looking through all the clouds and the darkness by which he is surrounded, ever through and through until there breaks upon his astonished vision the ultimate realization of all for which he has long hoped.

We know the pictures: Abraham on Moriah; Moses on the mountain with hands uplifted while Amalek fights Israel; Gideon acting to set his people free from Midianitish oppression; Jeremiah in the midst of utter failure, the prophet of failure; and Ezekiel in exile by the river banks.

Now all these men knew the meaning of my text and knew it in one particular way in each case. In connection with these five pictures I find the name illustrated. Abraham on Moriah said, "Jehovah-Jireh." Moses on the mountain said, "Jehovah-Nissi." Gideon facing the conflict said, "Jehovah-Shalom." Jeremiah in the dungeon heard the word, "Jehovah-Tsidkenu." And Ezekiel by the river said as the last thing in his prophecy "Jehovah-Shammah."

Jehovah-Jireh, the Lord will see and provide. Jehovah-Nissi, the Lord our banner. Jehovah-Shalom, the Lord our peace. Jehovah-Tsidkenu, the Lord our righteousness. Jehovah-Shammah, the Lord is there.

In these pictures, I find an interpretation of the meaning of my text which is full of value. "The name of the Lord is a strong tower: the righteous runneth into it, and is safe."

In the case of Abraham, we have an illustration of the obedience of faith in extremity. And by extremity I meant that he had come to the last test of his faith. Faith had been tried and tested and proved through all the years, but this was the final test. "Take now thy son, thine only son, whom thou lovest, even Isaac." All the promises of God were to be fulfilled in and through Isaac, and there was no other way in sight. Nevertheless, this man, in the hour of faith's stern and awful and overwhelming extremity, found the tower of refuge a place of strength, a high rock pinnacle where he was set above the stress and strain. "Jehovah-Jireh" means, quite literally, the Lord will see; but inferentially, and by intention, the Lord will provide. There is not a great distance between seeing and providing, vision and provision. Provision is the outcome of vision; and this man, when the command was given, and the altar was prepared, and he was at the end of everything upon which he had been leaning, did not say, "I cannot see"; but he said, "God can see"; and thus he ran into the tower of refuge. The Divine vision and provision was the place of strength to a man when his faith was obedient to the very last extremity of its testing.

Again, the picture of Moses upon the mountain is that of the conflict of faith. The hour had come when the men of faith, who had been redeemed because of their belief in Him Who had endured having seen Him Who is invisible, were gathered in conflict; and in the conflict Moses knew that everything depended not upon the strength of their fighting, but upon the presence and the power of God. In that hour he uttered these great words, "Jehovah-Nissi," the Lord our banner. I like to imagine the picture from Moses' standpoint. There in the valley are the hosts of Amalek—cruel, overwhelming hosts. And there also is this little company of fighting Israelites. But what did

Moses say that day when, conscious of the stress of the conflict, he ran in to the name of the Lord? Like a banner floating and fluttering in the breeze, he saw that name and knew the victory depended upon God's presence with them. The name of the Lord to him was a strong tower to which he ran and was set on high.

Or Gideon yonder is seen shrinking from service; and I have no criticism for him. I have already said that he was a farmer, a man of simple tastes, unused to the things of war. This man was apprehended and appointed, in the midst of his toil, to be the deliverer of the people from long and brutal and cruel oppression. Oh, how he shrank, afraid even of the vision of the angel that had come to him for his commissioning. He said, I have seen the angel of the Lord, and I shall die. It was then that the great word came, "Jehovah-Shalom," the Lord send peace. And he went into the name of God and was set on high above his own fears, above his own anxieties; and in that moment he became the intrepid leader who presently was content to fight with three hundred rather than thirty-two thousand because such was the revealed will and method and purpose of God.

Or, I go once more to that dungeon and see Jeremiah therein—a man who is the witness of faith in the midst of the most hopeless circumstances, and what is his hope? He says, "Jehovah-Tsidkenu," the Lord our righteousness. He knows perfectly well that there can be no civic strength that is not based on righteousness, no national restoration and uplifting that is not founded upon righteousness. And where is righteousness? Absent from the counsels of kings, absent from the policies of the men who were ruling, absent from the national leaders at that moment. Then he entered into the name of the Lord, "Jehovah-Tsidkenu," and was certain that because He was righteous the victory must be won; and he sang the song of the certainty thereof.

And, finally, Ezekiel by the Chebar, seeing his visions of God, was a man of faith in the hour of exile when all upon which human hope had been set was broken to a thousand pieces; and he saw through the mists and through the clouds, and as he looked to the ultimate, that on which he finally dwelt was not the glory of a temple or the prosperity of a people, but the presence of God. Ezekiel saw Jehovah present in the process, and consequently, present finally in the fulfillment of purpose. "The name of Jehovah is a strong tower."

The Proofs of Safety

I leave those illustrations, and I ask you for a moment to think with me of the proofs of safety. My brethren, all these I have referred to are in themselves proofs of how safe men are when they enter into this name. Abraham, Moses, Gideon, Jeremiah and Ezekiel; you notice that the illustrations coincide with the history of the nation. The whole history of Israel is in these illustrations. Abraham, the father and founder; Moses, the law-giver and leader; Gideon, the leader at a particular time of peril; Jeremiah, the prophet of failure; Ezekiel amid the failure. All these men were able to sing the song of victory, and to achieve a present victory, and pass its power on to coming days because they knew the strength of this great name. In every case these men were set on high above the tumult and the stress, entering into the place of peace even in the midst of conflict.

The Bible abounds with illustrations. Daniel knew conflict; he was persecuted, and they took him and put him in the den of lions. But if you tell me that Daniel was in the den of lions you have discovered only the most superficial truth. Where then was Daniel? In the name of Jehovah, in the den of lions; and when the king in the morning said, "O, Daniel, servant of the living God, is thy God, Whom thou servest continually, able to deliver thee from the lions?" Daniel answered, "O, king, live forever. My God hath sent His angel, and hath shut the lions' mouths." He went into the tower and was set on high.

Or Job, who came to the fulfillment of his own life when he found his way through the flaming glory of the Theophany into the secret place of the name and rested therein.

Or David, if indeed the psalm we read this morning

was David's psalm. Did you notice the growth of experience and the growth of the sense of safety? At the beginning of the psalm he said, "I shall not be greatly moved" (Ps. 62:2), but before the song was done he said, "I shall not be moved" (v. 6). And how did he climb from trembling confidence to matchless assurance? Read the psalm again, and it will be seen that it is the psalm of God and the song of the name of the Lord—the song of a soul gathering courage and heroism in the secret place.

We need not confine ourselves to biblical illustration. "Saints, apostles, prophets, martyrs," who passed through conflicts as severe, if not severer, than we can ever know, put their trust in this name and found it safe. Or may I not appeal to some of you who are in the midst of conflict to prove the assertion of the text by the memory of things you have known in the lives of your loved ones? Will you let me help you by an illustration? I remember, seven and thirty years ago, when God took from my side—the side of an only boy—his one playmate, his sister. Do not ever indulge in the heresy that a child is incapable of sorrow. I remember coming back one morning—only a lad as I then was—from the grave where I had sat in loneliness, and I found in the house my father and mother. And, boy as I was, I crept up to where they were sitting together, and, if you like the heathenism of the word, it happened—there is a better word than that— my father's hand was resting on his Bible, and I looked at where his finger rested, and I saw these words: "The Lord gave, and the Lord hath taken away: blessed be the name of the Lord." And, boy as I was, I knew there was a connection between that verse and the light I saw on the faces of father and mother; and I never lost the impression of it. And, twenty-four years after, when my own first little girl was taken out of my own home, I got the Bible and turned up the same verse, and laid my hand where my father had laid his hand. "The name of the Lord is a strong tower: The righteous runneth into it, and is set on high."

The proof is scattered through the experience of the saints in all the ages and is as near to you as father and mother's trust in God. Nay, verily, brethren, have you not yourselves proved it?

Of the supreme onslaught and victory, we have the story in the New Testament. Jesus knew the conflict of life as none other has ever known it. He knew the forces of spiritual antagonism. He lived in the midst of the problems that vex us. And the subtle forms of temptation with which we are familiar, He knew them and entered deeply and profoundly into them. He knew the sorrows of bereavement and difficulty; He was a man of sorrows and acquainted with grief. And how did He overcome them? To Him the name of the Lord was a strong tower into which He passed and was set on high. The supreme secret of all His victory over sin and sorrow is contained in His own confession, "I and My Father are one." In fellowship with Him He overcame.

But there is a deeper significance in that story of Jesus. The name Jesus in itself is composed of the ancient name Jehovah, and yet another word that speaks of salvation. The name Jesus essentially means "Jehovah is salvation." The name Jesus is Joshua. Now let my young friends take their Bibles and find out when the name was made. The Son of Nun did not bear it first. It was given to him. The significance is that of Jehovah and salvation interwoven, making the name Joshua which is our name Jesus; and into that name finally we may run and be set on high.

> Jesus, name of sweetness,
>   Jesus, sound of love,
> Cheering exiles onward
>   To their rest above.

My brethren, what is the conflict to you this morning? Are you at the extremity of faith? Are you asked to walk a pathway that seems as though it must end in disaster? Are you sure it is God's will? Then, in comradeship with this Christ Who walked the *via dolorosa* and walked the way to victory, take your way along that pathway. Are you in conflict with foes in the valley that are against faith and against God? Let your hands be uplifted, and in that name Jesus there is a banner of Jehovah and victory must come as you follow Him. Are you commissioned to some work from which you shrink as did Gideon of old? In Jesus is the fulfillment of the great word "Jehovah-Shalom," for He is our peace; and we may enter into all service in perfect peace in Him.

Are you feeling, rightly or wrongly, that you are strangely in company with Jeremiah, that all the foundations are breaking down around you, and that the national outlook is of the darkest? I pray you, in your dungeon, look higher and see "Jehovah-Tsidkenu." Or, if you would translate it into modern language, sing this: "Jesus shall reign where'er the sun/doth his successive journeys run." And if today the thickening battle and the darkening gloom overwhelm you, stay a little by the river and look far enough and earnestly enough, and beyond all the mystery of the hour you will see the glory of God's victory; and its chief word is this, "Jehovah-Shammah," the Lord is there. The crowned Christ, having won the kingdoms of the world, will make them His own to the glory of God.

The Good Shepherd

Charles Haddon Spurgeon (1834-1892) is undoubtedly the most famous minister of modern times. Converted in 1850, he united with the Baptists and soon began to preach in various places. He became pastor of the Baptist church in Waterbeach in 1851, and three years later he was called to the decaying Park Street Church, London. Within a short time, the work began to prosper, a new church was built and dedicated in 1861, and Spurgeon became London's most popular preacher. In 1855, he began to publish his sermons weekly; and today they make up the fifty-seven volumes of *The Metropolitan Tabernacle Pulpit*. He founded a pastor's college and several orphanages.

This sermon is taken from *The Metropolitan Tabernacle Pulpit*, Volume 53.

Charles Haddon Spurgeon

11

THE GOOD SHEPHERD

The Lord is my shepherd; I shall not want (Psalm 23:1).

DOES NOT THIS sound just like poetry or like singing? If you read the entire Psalm through, it is written in such poetic prose that, though it is not translated into meter as it should have been, it reads just like it. "The Lord is my Shepherd; I shall not want. He maketh me to lie down in green pastures; he leadeth me beside the still waters. He restoreth my soul: he leadeth me in the paths of righteousness for his name's sake." It sounds like music for this, among other reasons, because it came from David's heart. That which comes from the heart always has melody in it. When men speak of what they do know and from the depths of their souls testify to what they have seen, they speak with what we call eloquence for true eloquence is speaking from the soul. Thus David spoke of what he knew, what he had verified all his life long, and this rendered him truly eloquent.

As "truth is stranger than fiction," so the truth that David spoke is sweeter than even fancy could have imagined; and it has more beauty than even the dream of the enthusiast could have pictured. "The Lord is my Shepherd; I shall not want." How naturally it seems to strike on the ear as uttered by David who had himself been a shepherd boy! He remembers how he had led his flock by the waters in the warm summer; how he had made them lie down in shady nooks by the side of the river; how, on sultry days, he had led them on the high hills that they might feel the cool air; and how, when the winter set in, he had led them into the valleys that they might be hidden from the stormy blast; well could he remember the tender care with which he protected the lambs, and carried them; and how he had tended the wounded of the

143

flock. And now, appropriating to himself the familiar figure of a sheep, he says, "The Lord is my Shepherd; I shall not want." I will try to preach experimentally tonight, and I wonder how many of you will be able to follow the psalmist with me while I attempt to do so.

First of all, *there are some preliminaries* before a man can say this: it is absolutely necessary that he should feel himself to be like a sheep by nature for he cannot know that God is his Shepherd unless he feels in himself that he has the nature of a sheep. Secondly, *there is a sweet assurance*; a man must have had some testimony of divine care and goodness in the past, otherwise he cannot appropriate to himself this verse, "The Lord is my Shepherd." And thirdly, *there is a holy confidence.* I wonder how many there are here who can place all their future in the hand of God and can join with David in uttering the last sentence, "The Lord is my Shepherd; I shall not want."

First, then, we say

There Is a Certain Confession Necessary Before a Man Can Join in These Words

We must feel that there is something in us which is akin to the sheep; we must acknowledge that, in some measure, we exactly resemble it, or else we cannot call God our Shepherd.

I think the first apprehension we shall have, if the Lord has brought us into this condition, is this—we shall be conscious of our own folly; we shall feel how unwise we always are. *A sheep is one of the most unwise of creatures.* It will go anywhere except in the right direction; it will leave a fat pasture to wander into a barren one; it will find out many ways, but not the right way; it would wander through a wood and find its way through ravines into the wolf's jaws, but never by its wariness turn away from the wolf; it could wander near his den, but it would not instinctively turn aside from the place of danger; it knows how to go astray, but it knows not how to come home again. Left to itself, it would not know in what pasture to feed in summer or whither to retire in winter.

Have we ever been brought to feel that, in matters or

providence as well as in things of grace, we are truly and entirely foolish? Methinks, no man can trust providence till he distrusts himself; and no one can say, "The Lord is my Shepherd, I shall not want," until he has given up every idle notion that he can control himself or manage his own interest. Alas! we are most of us wise above that which is written, and we are too vain to acknowledge the wisdom of God. In our self-esteem, we fancy our reason can rule our purposes, and we never doubt our own power to accomplish our own intentions, and then, by a little maneuvering, we think to extricate ourselves from our difficulties. Could we steer in such a direction as we have planned, we entertain not a doubt that we should avoid at once the Scylla and the Charybodis and have fair sailing all our life long. O beloved, surely it needs but little teaching in the school of grace to make out that we are fools. True wisdom is sure to set folly in a strong light.

I have heard of a young man who went to college; and when he had been there a year, his father said to him, "Do you know more than when you went?" "Oh, yes!" said he, "I do." Then he went the second year and was asked the same question, "Do you know more than when you went?" "Oh, no!" said he, "I know a great deal less." "Well," said the father, "you are getting on." Then he went the third year and was asked, "What do you know now?" "Oh!" said he, "I don't think I know anything." "That is right," said the father; "you have now learned to profit, since you say you know nothing."

He who is convinced that he knows nothing as he ought to know gives up steering his ship and lets God put His hand on the rudder. He lays aside his own wisdom and cries, "O God, my little wisdom is cast at Thy feet. Such as it is, I surrender it to you. I am prepared to renounce it for it has caused me many an ill and many a tear of regret that I should have followed my own devices, but henceforth I will delight in Your statutes. As the eyes of servants look unto the hand of their masters and as the eyes of a maiden unto the hand of her mistress, so shall mine eyes wait upon the Lord my God. I will not trust in horses or in chariots; but the name of the God of Jacob shall be my refuge. Too long, alas! have I sought my own pleasure and labored to do everything for my own gratification. Now would I ask, O Lord, Your help that I may seek first the kingdom of God and His righteousness and leave all the rest to you."

Do you, O my friends, feel persuaded that you are foolish? Have you been brought to confess the sheepishness of your nature? Or are you flattering your hearts with the fond conceit that you are wise? If so, you are indeed fools. But if brought to see yourself like Agur when he said, "I am more brutish than any man, and have not the understanding of a man," then even Solomon might pronounce you wise. And if you are thus brought to confess, "I am a silly sheep," I hope you will be able to say, "The Lord is my Shepherd, I cannot have any other, I want none other; He is enough for me."

Again, a sheep is not only foolish, but *it is a very dependent creature.* The sheep, at least in its domesticated state as we know it, must ever be dependent. If we should take a horse, we might turn him loose upon the prairie, and there he would find sufficient for his sustenance; and, years later, we might see him in no worse condition than that in which we left him. Even the ox might thus be treated and still be able to provide for itself. But as for the silly sheep, set it alone in the wilderness, let it pursue its own course unheeded, and what would be its fate? Presently, if it did not wander into places where it would be starved, it would ultimately come to ruin for assuredly some wild beast would lay hold upon it, and it has no way to defend itself.

Beloved, have we been brought to feel that we have of ourselves no means of subsistence and no power of defense against our foes? Do we perceive the necessity for our dependence upon God? If so, then we have learned another part of the great lesson that the Lord is our Shepherd. Some of us have yet this lesson to learn. We would cater for ourselves and carve for ourselves; but, as the good old Puritan says, "No child of God ever carves for himself without cutting his fingers." We sometimes fancy that we can do a little for ourselves; but we shall have that conceit taken out of us very soon. If we indeed be God's people, He will bring us to depend absolutely upon Him day by day. He will make us pray, "Give us *this* day our daily bread," and make us acknowledge that He opens His hand and gives us our meat in due season. Sweet is the meal that we eat, as it were, out of His hand.

Yet some will rebel against this dependence as very humiliating. Men like to vaunt their independence; nothing is more respectable in their eyes than to live in independent circumstances. But it is no use for us to talk of being independent; we never can be. I remember a dear Christian man who prayed very sweetly each Sunday morning at a certain prayer-meeting that I once attended, "O Lord, we are *independent* creatures upon Thee." Except in such a sense as that, I never knew any independence worth having. Of course, he meant, "we are *de*pendent creatures upon Thee." So we must be. We cannot be independent even of one another, and certainly we are not independent of God; for, when we have health and strength, we are dependent upon Him for their continuance; and if we have them not, we are dependent on Him to restore them to us.

In all matters whatsoever, it is sweet, it is blessed, to see the tokens of His watchful care. If I had a thing of which I could say, "God has not given me this," I hope, by divine grace, I should turn it out of doors. Food, raiment, health, breath, strength, everything comes from Him, and we are constantly dependent upon Him. As Huntington used to say, "My God gives me a hand-basket portion. He does not give me an abundance at once; but He gives it basket by basket, and I live from hand to mouth." Or, as old Hardy once said, "I am a gentleman commoner on the bounty of God; I live day by day upon morning commons and evening commons; and thus I am dependent upon Him, independent of the world, but dependent upon God." The sheep is a dependent creature always needing some help; and so is the Christian; and he realizes the blessedness of his dependence when he can say, "The Lord is my Shepherd."

These are the two principal points upon which we view

this truth with regard to providence. I might wander from what I wished to be the subject of this evening, and I might be doing good if I were to show you some other points of comparison between the Christian and the sheep. O beloved, there are some of you here present who know yourselves to be sheep *by reason of your frequent wanderings.* How often have we made this confession, "We have erred and strayed from thy ways like lost sheep," and we do feel it this night, bitterly ruing the waywardness of our hearts. But it is well to be the sheep of God's pasture even if we have been wandering sheep. We do not read of wandering dogs because dogs are naturally wild while sheep are always accounted to be someone's property. The straying sheep has an owner; and however far it may stray from the fold, it ceases not to belong to that owner. I believe that God will yet bring back into the fold every one of His own sheep, and they shall all be saved. It is something to feel our wanderings; for if we feel ourselves to be lost, we shall certainly be saved; if we feel ourselves to have wandered, we shall certainly be brought back.

Again, we are just like sheep *by reason of the perverseness of our wills.* People talk about free-will Christians and tell us of persons being saved and coming to God of their own free will. It is a very curious thing, but though I have heard a great many free-will sermons, I never heard any free-will prayers. I have heard Arminianism in preaching and talking, but I have never heard any Arminian praying. In fact, I do not think there can be any prayer of that sort; it is a style that does not suit prayer. The theory may look very nice in argument and sound very proper in discourse though we somewhat differ from it; but for practical purposes it is useless. The language will not suit us in prayer, and this alone would be sufficient reason to condemn it.

If a man cannot pray in the spirit of his own convictions, it shows they are a delusion from beginning to end; for if they were true, he could pray in that language as well as in any other. Blessed be God, the doctrines of grace are as good to pray with as to preach with! We do not find ourselves out of order in any act of worship when once we have the old fundamental doctrines of the blessed gospel of grace. Persons talk about free-will Christians coming back to Jesus of themselves. I intend to believe them when they find me a free-will sheep that has come back of itself or when they have discovered some sheep, asking to be taken in again. You will not find such a sheep, and you will not find a free-will Christian; for they will all confess, if you thoroughly probe the matter, that it was grace and grace alone that restored their souls. It was—

> Grace taught our souls to pray,
>   And made our eyes o'er flow;
> 'Tis grace that keeps us to this day,
>   And will not let us go.

The second thing is,

The Assurance That the Lord Is Our Shepherd

It is very easy to say, "The Lord is *a* Shepherd"; but how shall we appropriate the blessedness to ourselves and be able to say, "The Lord is *our* Shepherd"? I answer that He has had certain dealings with our souls in the past which have taught us that He is our Shepherd. If every man and every woman in this assembly should rise up and say, "The Lord is my Shepherd," I feel convinced it would be, in many instances, the solemn utterance of an untruth; for there are, it is to be feared, many here who have not God for their Shepherd. He is their Guide, it is true in some sense, because He overrules all the hearts and controls all the affairs of the children of men; but they are not the people of His pasture, they are not the sheep of His hand; they do not believe, therefore they are not of His fold. And if some of you should say that you are, your own conscience would belie you. How, then, does a man come to know that the Lord is his Shepherd?

He knows it, first, *because Jesus Christ has brought him back from his wanderings.* If there be anyone here who, after a course of folly and sin, has been fetched back from the mountains of error and the haunts of evil, if there be one here who has been stopped in a mad career of vice and has been reclaimed by the power of Jehovah Jesus, such an one will know by a happy experience that the Lord is his Shepherd. If I once wandered on yon mountaintop, and Jesus climbed up, and caught me, and put me on His shoulders, and carried me home, I cannot and dare not doubt that He is my Shepherd. If I had belonged to some other sheep-owner, he would not have sought me; and from the fact that He did seek me, I learn that He must be my Shepherd. Did I think that any man convinced me of sin or that any human power had converted me, I should fear I was that man's sheep and that he was my shepherd. Could I trace my deliverance to the hand of the creature, I should think that a creature might be my shepherd; but, since he who has been reclaimed of God must and will confess that God alone has done it and will ascribe to His free grace and to that alone his deliverance from sin, such an one will feel persuaded that the Lord must be his Shepherd because He fetched him back from his wanderings, He snatched him out of the jaw of the lion and out of the paw of the bear.

We know still further that, like a shepherd, *he has supplied our wants.* Some of you, beloved, know of a surety that God is your Provider. You have been brought, sometimes, into such straits that if it had not been for an interposition of heaven itself, you never could have had deliverance. You have sunk so deep down into poverty, and lovers and acquaintances have stood so far aloof from you that you know there is but one arm which could have fetched you up. You have been reduced, perhaps, to such straits that all you could do was to pray. You have wrestled at the throne and sought for an answer, but it has not come; you have used every effort to extricate yourself and still darkness has compassed your path. Again and again you have tried till hope well-nigh vanished from your heart, and then, adding vows to your prayer, you have said in your agony, "O God, if You will deliver me this time, I will never doubt again!"

Look back on the path of your pilgrimage. Some of you can count as many Ebenezers as there are milestones from here to York; Ebenezers piled up with oil poured on the top of them; places where you have said, "Hitherto the Lord hath helped me." Look through the pages of your diary, and you will see time after time when your perils and exigencies were such as no earthly skill could relieve, and you felt constrained to witness what others among you have never felt—that there is a God, that there is a providence—a God who compasses your path and is acquainted with all your ways. You have received deliverance in so marvelous a way from so unseen a hand and so unlikely a source under circumstances, perhaps, so foreign to your wishes, and yet the deliverance has been so perfect, so complete, and wonderful that you have been obliged to say, "The Lord *is* my Shepherd." Yes; *He is.*

The sheep, we know, fed day by day in good pasture, may forget its shepherd; but if, for a time, it is taken from the pasture and then brought home again after having been nearly starved, it says, "Truly, He is my Shepherd." If I had always been supplied with bread without the pinch of anxiety, I might have doubted whether He had given it and ascribed it to the ordinary course of passing events; but, seeing that "everywhere and in all things I am instructed both to be full and to be hungry, both to abound and to suffer need," I own that it is my God who supplies all my need; yea, and with gratitude I will write it down for a certainty, "The Lord is my Shepherd."

But, beloved, do not be distressed even though you should not have had these particular trials and deliverances for there is a way whereby we can tell the Lord is our Shepherd without encountering so many rough and rugged passes as I will show you presently. I have heard it said by some that a man cannot be a child of God unless he has gone through a certain set of trials and troubles. I recollect hearing a sermon from these words, "Who passing through the valley of Baca make it a well." Certainly, the preacher did not make his sermon a well for it was as dry as a stick and not worth hearing. There was nothing like cheerfulness in it; but a flood of declamation all the way through against hopeful Christians, against people going to heaven who are not always grumbling, and murmuring, and doubting, fumbling for their evidences amidst the exercises of their own hearts, ever reading and striving to rival Job and Jeremiah in grief, taking the Lamentations as the fit expression of their own lips, troubling their poor brains and vexing their poor hearts, and smarting, and crying, and wearying themselves with the perpetual habit of complaining against God, saying with poor Job, "My stroke is heavier than my groaning." Such persons measure themselves by their troubles, and trials, and distresses, and tribulations, and perplexities, and no end of these things that we will not stop to recount.

We believe, indeed, that such things will come to a child of God; we think every Christian will be corrected in due measure; we should be the last to deny that God's people are a tried people. They must all pass through the furnace of affliction, and He has chosen them there; but, still, we believe that religion is a blessed and a happy thing, and we love to sing that verse—

> The men of grace have found
>   Glory begun below;
> Celestial fruits on earthly ground
>   From faith and hope may grow.

And what though some of my hearers have not yet had to swim through the rivers, though they may not have had to pass through the fiery furnace of providential trial, they have had trials enough, and trials that no heart has known except their own, sufferings which they could not tell to flesh and blood which have gnawed their very souls and entered into the marrow of their spirits; bitter anguish and aching voids such as those who boast about their trials never felt, such as mere babbling troublers did never know, deep rushings of the stream of woe with which little bubbling narrow brooks could never compare. Such persons fear to murmur, they cannot tell their sufferings because they think it would be showing some want of trust in God; they keep their trials to themselves and only tell them into that ear which hears and has no lips to babble afterward.

"But," you say, "how can you tell that the Lord is your

Shepherd if you have not been tried in any of those great deeps?" We know that He is *because He has fed us day by day in good pasture.* And if He has not suffered us to wander so far away as others, we can lift up our eyes to Him, and each one of us say, "Lord, You are my Shepherd; I can as fully prove that You are my Shepherd by Your keeping me in the grassy field as by Your fetching me back when I have wandered; I know You are as much my Shepherd when You have supplied my wants day by day as if You had suffered me to go into poverty and given me bitterness; I know You are as much my Shepherd when granting me a continual stream of mercy as if that stream had stopped for a moment and then had begun to flow again."

Some people say, if they have had an accident and been nearly killed or have narrowly escaped, "What a providence!" Yet it is as much a providence when you have no accident at all. A good man once went to a certain place to meet his son. Both he and his son had ridden from some distance. When the son arrived, he exclaimed, "Oh father! I had such a providence on the road." "Why, what was that?" "My horse stumbled six times, and yet I was not thrown." "Dear me!" said his father, "but I have had a providence too." "And what was that?" "Why, my horse never stumbled at all, and that is just as much a providence as if the horse had stumbled six times, and I had not been thrown."

It is a great providence when you have lost your property, and God provides for you; but it is quite as much a providence when you have no loss at all and when you are still able to live above the depths of penury; and so God provides for you. I say this to some of you whom God has blessed and continually provided for from your earliest youth; you, too, can each of you say, "The Lord is my Shepherd." You can see this title stamped on your mercies; though they come daily, they are given to you by God; and you will say, by humble faith, the word *"my"* as loudly as anyone can. Do not get despising the little ones of the flock because they have not had so many trials as you have had; do not get cutting the children of God in pieces because they have not been in such fights as you have. The Shepherd leads the sheep where He pleases, and be sure that He will lead them rightly; and as long as they can say from their hearts, "The Lord is my Shepherd, I shall not want," do not trouble yourselves about where or how they learned it.

Finally, look at

The Holy Confidence of the Psalmist: "I shall not want"

"There," poor unbelief says, "I am wanting in everything; I am wanting in spirituals, I am wanting in temporals; and I shall want. Ah! such distress as I had a little while ago; you cannot tell what it was; it was enough to break one's heart; and it is coming again; I *shall* want." That is what you say, unbelief, but you must write your own name at the bottom, and then I will repeat to you this, "The Lord is my Shepherd, I shall not want." That is what David said, and I think David's faith far preferable to your unbelief. I might take your evidence in some matters, but I really would not take it before David's. I would accept your testimony as an honest man in some respects, but the words of inspiration must be preferable to your words of apprehension. When I find it written, "The Lord is my Shepherd, I shall not want," I would rather take one of David's affirmations than fifty of your negations.

Methinks I hear someone saying, "I would bear the want of any temporal good if I could but obtain spiritual blessings. I am in want this night of more faith, more love, more holiness, more communion with my Savior." Well, beloved, the Lord is your Shepherd. You shall not want even these blessings; if you ask of Him, He will give them to you though it may be by terrible things in righteousness that He will save you. He often answers His people in an unexpected manner; many of God's answers to our letters come down in black-edged envelopes; yet, mark you, they will come. If you want peace, joy, sanctification, and such blessings, they shall be given to you for God has promised them.

The Lord is your Shepherd, you shall not want. I have

often thought of that great promise written in the Bible—I do not know where there is a larger one—"No good thing will he withhold from them that walk uprightly." "No good thing!" It is a mercy that the word "good" was put in, for if it had said, "He will withhold nothing," we should have been asking for many things that would be bad for us; but it says, "no good thing"! Now, spiritual mercies are good things, and not only good things but the best things, so that you may well ask for them; for if no good thing will be withheld, much more will none of the best things. Ask, then, Christian, for He is your Shepherd, and you shall not want; He will supply your need; He will give you whatever you require; ask in faith, nothing doubting, and He will give you what you really need.

But still there are some who say, "The text applies to temporal matters," and persist in it. Well, then, I will accept this sense—the Lord is your Shepherd, you shall not want for temporal blessings. "Ah!" cries one, "I was once in affluence, and now I am brought down to penury. I once stood among the mighty and was rich, now I walk amongst the lowly and am poor." Well, David does not say, "The Lord is your Shepherd, and you shall not come down in society"; he does not say, "The Lord is your Shepherd, and therefore you shall have five hundred or a thousand pounds a year"; he does not say, "The Lord is your Shepherd, and therefore you shall have whatsoever your soul lusts after." All David says is, "The Lord is my Shepherd; I shall not want."

There are different ways of wanting. There are many people whose foolish craving and restless anxiety make them always in want. If you gave them a house to live in and fed them day by day, they would always be wanting something more. And after you had just relieved their necessities, they would want still. The fact is, theirs are not real wants but simply fancied wants. David does not say, "The Lord is my Shepherd, therefore I shall not fancy that I want"; for though God might promise that, it would need His omnipotence to carry it out for His people often get fancying that they want when they do not. It is real wants that are referred to. "The Lord is my Shepherd; I shall not really want." There are many things we wish for that we do not really need, but there is no promise given that we shall have all we wish for.

God has not said that He would give us anything more than we need, but He will give us that. So, lift up your head, and do not be afraid. Fear not, God is with you; He shall prevent evil from hurting you; He shall turn darkness into light and bitter into sweet. All the way He has led you, and all the way He shall lead you; this shall be your constant joy. He is my Shepherd, I shall not really want that which is absolutely necessary. Whatever I really require shall be given by the lavish hand of a tender Father. Believer, here is your inheritance, here is your income, here is your yearly living: "He is your Shepherd, and you shall not want." What is your income, believer? "Why," you say, "it varies with some and others of us." Well, but a believer's income is still the same. This is it: "The Lord is my Shepherd, I shall not want." That is my income, and it is yours, poor little one. That is the income of the poorest pauper in the workhouse who has an interest in the grace of God; the Lord is her Shepherd, she shall not want. That is the income of the poor foundling child who has come to know the Lord in early life and has no other friend; the Lord is his Shepherd, he shall not want. That is the widow's inheritance; the Lord is her Shepherd, she shall not want. That is the orphan's fortune; the Lord is his Shepherd, he shall not want. That is the believer's portion, his inheritance, his blessing. *

"Well now," some may say, "what is this truth worth?" Beloved, if we could change this truth for a world of gold, we would not; we had rather live on this truth than live on the finest fortune in creation; we reckon that this is an inheritance that makes us rich indeed; "The Lord is my Shepherd; I shall not want." Give me ten thousand pounds, and one reverse of fortune may scatter it all away; but let me have a spiritual hold of this divine assurance, "The Lord is my Shepherd, I shall not want," then I am set up for life. I cannot break with such stock as this in hand; I never can be a bankrupt for I hold this security: "The Lord is my Shepherd; I shall not want." Do not give me ready money now; give me a checkbook, and let me draw what I like. That is what God does with the believer. He does what I like. That is what God does with the believer. He does not immediately transfer His inheritance to him, but lets him draw what he needs out of the riches of his fullness in Christ Jesus.

The Lord is his Shepherd; he shall not want. What a glorious inheritance! Walk up and down it, Christian; lie down upon it, it will do for your pillow; it will be soft as down for you to lie upon: "The Lord is my Shepherd; I shall not want." Climb up that creaking staircase to the top of thy house, lie down on your hard mattress, wrap yourself round with a blanket, look out for the winter when hard times are coming, and say not, "What shall I do?" but just hum over to yourself these words, "The Lord is my Shepherd; I shall not want." That will be like the hush of a lullaby to your poor soul, and you will soon sink to slumber. Go, business man, to your counting-house again after this little hour of recreation in God's house, and again cast up those wearisome books. You are saying, "How about business? These prices may be my ruin. What shall I do?" When you have cast up your accounts, put this down against all your fears and see what a balance it will leave, "The Lord is my Shepherd; I shall not want."

There is another man. He does not lack anything, but still he feels that some great loss may injure him considerably. Go and write this down in your cash-book. If you have made out your cash-account truly, put this down: "The Lord is my Shepherd; I shall not want." Put this down for something better than dollars and cents, something better than gold and silver: "The Lord is my Shepherd; I shall not want." He who disregards this truth knows nothing about its preciousness, but he who apprehends it says, "Ah ye, it is true, The Lord is my Shepherd; I shall not want.'" He will find this promise like Chian wine, of which the ancients said that it was flavored to the lip of him that tasted it; so this truth shall taste sweet to you if your spiritual palate is pure, yet it shall be worth nothing to you but mere froth if your taste is not healthy.

But, beloved, we must divide our congregation before we send you away and remind you that there are some of you to whom this truth does not belong. Perhaps some of you professors of religion may want this truth badly enough; but it is not yours. The Lord is not your Shepherd; you are not the sheep of His pasture and the flock of His hand. You are not the sheep, but goats—unclean creatures, not harmless and undefiled as sheep, but everything that is the very reverse. Oh! it is not only eternal loss, it is not only everlasting injury that you have to regret—it is also present loss and present injury, the loss of a jointure on earth, the loss of an inheritance below. To be deprived of such a comfort as this is a terrible privation. Oh! it is enough to make men long for religion if it were only for that sweet placidity and calm of mind which it gives here below.

Well might men wish for this heavenly oil to be cast on the troubled waters of this mortal life even if they did not anoint their heads therewith and enter into glory with the joy of their Lord upon their countenance. Beloved, there are some I know here—and your conscience tells you whom I mean—who have a voice within your own hearts which says, "I am not one of Christ's sheep." Well then, there is no promise for you that you shall not want; the promise and the providence are for believers, not for you. There is no promise that all things shall work together for your good; but rather, cursed shall you be in your basket and cursed in your goings out and in your comings in for "the curse of the Lord is in the house of the wicked." It does not merely peep in at his window, but it is in his house. Yet God "blesseth the habitation of the just."

If you do not repent, the curse shall follow you until your dying day, and not having Christ for your Shepherd, you shall wander where the hungry wolf, the devil, shall at last seize upon your soul, and everlasting misery and destruction from the presence of Jehovah must be your inevitable, miserable, and inexpressibly awful doom. May the Lord in mercy deliver you from it! And this is the way of salvation: "He that believeth and is baptized shall be saved; but he that believeth not shall be damned." "He that believeth and is baptized"—we omit nothing that God has said. "He that believeth and is baptized"—not he that is baptized and then believeth (which would be reversing God's order), but "He that believeth and is baptized"—not he that is baptized without believing, but the two joined together—he that believeth with his heart and is baptized, confessing with his mouth—"he that believeth and is baptized shall be saved."

Do you neglect one part of it? It is at your peril, sir! "He that believeth and is baptized," says God. If any of you have neglected one portion of it, if you have believed and have not been baptized, God will save you. Still, this promise says not so. "He that believeth and is baptized"; it puts the two together; and "what God hath joined together, let no man put asunder"; what He has ordered let no man disarrange. "He that believeth"—that is, he who trusts in Jesus; he who relies upon His blood, His merits, and His righteousness—"and is baptized, shall be saved; but he that believeth not shall be damned."